THE HOME UNIVERSITY LIBRARY
OF MODERN KNOWLEDGE

125

ENGLAND UNDER THE
TUDORS AND STUARTS
1485-1688

EDITORS OF
The Home University Library
of Modern Knowledge

GILBERT MURRAY, O.M., D.C.L., F.B.A.

G. N. CLARK, D.LITT., F.B.A.

G. R. DE BEER, D.SC., F.R.S.

England under the Tudors and Stuarts
1485-1688

KEITH FEILING
O.B.E., D.Litt.

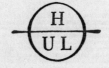

Geoffrey Cumberlege
OXFORD UNIVERSITY PRESS
LONDON   NEW YORK   TORONTO

First published in 1927, *and reprinted in* 1931, 1935,
1942, 1945, 1949 *and* 1951

PRINTED IN GREAT BRITAIN

CONTENTS

CHAP.		PAGE
I	INTRODUCTION	7
II	THE END OF THE MIDDLE AGES, 1485–1527	18
III	HENRY VIII AND THE REFORMATION	41
IV	THE DECIDING YEARS, 1547–61	66
V	THE ELIZABETHAN AGE	86
VI	CHURCH AND STATE	110
VII	THE FIRST TWO STUARTS, 1603–42	128
VIII	THE CIVIL WARS, 1642–9	148
IX	COMMONWEALTH AND PROTECTORATE	165
X	CHARLES II	183
XI	JAMES II AND THE FALL OF THE MONARCHY	209
XII	THE INTELLECTUAL BACKGROUND	230
	BIBLIOGRAPHY	252
	INDEX	254

ENGLAND UNDER THE TUDORS AND STUARTS

I

INTRODUCTORY

THE two centuries stretching between 1485 and 1688 can never become indifferent to the people of England, for in them modern England was made. The change from the Middle Ages was accomplished with startling rapidity. At the opening of the period national security was still threatened by nobles ruling whole counties with armed vassals, or by pretenders to the throne, financed from foreign States. Cardinals of the universal Church, their crosses borne before their barges on the Thames, dominated the Councils of the Crown; Convocation was still voting subsidies to crusades against the Turk; a thousand abbeys, friaries, and nunneries, held perhaps one-tenth of English soil. The fabric of government was still medieval. The King in Council carried on the everyday work of administration; intervals of five years often elapsed between the meetings of Parliament. Economically, men of average means lived in much isolation. Each manor produced two-thirds of its needs; guilds and crafts traded mainly in local markets. England as a power in Europe was little advanced since the days of the Black Prince; Calais was still English, and France the old rival. The keys of commerce were still turned by Venice, Flanders, and the Hanse Towns. The Cape of Good Hope was not yet rounded, America as yet only a traveller's tale. The world seemed to be fixed so fast that it could not be moved, and the horizons of men's minds were flat and narrow. Though Caxton had already printed some fifty books, the new art had not yet reached the stage of common use, and the Court poets and chroniclers of the first Tudor, the theology of his bishops, or the popular drama that he yawned over on his progresses, were still Catholic, wooden, and conventional. If the fifteenth century had been by no means a prison-house, it had been little more than a preparatory school, where pioneer efforts to break out of fixed habits had been rigorously repressed, and where the doom for the heretic or iconoclast had been the stake or wholesale execution.

By 1688 the England in which we live had been, in bare essentials, created, and the problems of William III turned upon Cabinet government, a weekly Press, organized Nonconformity, capitalism, and an empire overseas. Whatever else came of those complicated processes labelled " Renaissance " and " Reformation," their effect was to sweep away, first in men's minds and then from the earth, the checks, balances, and restrictions which had made a communal life possible in the Middle Ages. The State and individual liberty grew up together—the lion with the lamb. When castle, manor, and guild broke down, the individual turned to a central power for direction and defence, while the young State appealed to the growing wealth of the individual bourgeois against relics of feudalism, fetters of Rome, or threats from new monarchies of Europe. The revival of classical teaching gave to both State and individual a brilliant justification for their revived existence; the religious Reformation cast over them the mantle of the spirit. By 1560, amid the dust of demolished medievalism, two mighty forces in England stood erect, two things, their champions claimed, each in some sense divine and elemental—the power of the State and the liberty of man.

One generation had been enough for this
mighty change, the lever of which had been a
public opinion multiplied by the printing-
press. To this both the sovereigns and their
critics appealed. Henry VIII combated revolt
as much by imperious proclamations as by
force of arms, and clinched his Reformation
by sending the English Bible to every parish.
Protestants and Catholics issued libels against
their rivals, or ballads to honour their martyrs.
Elizabethan secretaries and members of Parliament analyzed in print the institutions they
administered. The pamphlet did the work
both of newspaper and magazine, and one book-
seller's collection of thirty thousand during
the Civil War may give some idea of the
earlier output. Thames-bank was full of
theatres playing to popular audiences;
dramatic companies toured the provinces;
Burghley " tuned " the theatres to attack
Catholic and Puritan.

This intellectual ferment could not leave
untouched the centre of English life, and in
Elizabeth's later parliaments we may see
already the future controversies of Church and
State, under discussion by a trained political
class, whose arguments prepare us for the
division between Whig and Tory.

A new ruling class of squires, lawyers, and

merchants controlled this volume of public opinion. Their instinct of order had rescued the Tudors from rebels. To them were distributed the riches of the Church, to them committed the tasks of local government, that fell from the hands of nobility or guilds. National wealth bounded forward under the impetus of prolonged peace, of divisions among our European foes, and of new markets in distant seas. Dismissing the memory of castles in Aquitaine, at last we went down to our proper element, the ocean. The riches forthcoming from our voyages broke down all barriers set up in former times against usury, enterprise, and competition, and capitalist society arose. By Elizabeth's death the most fertile land was enclosed in private ownership, stocks and shares were changing hands on the London exchange, syndicates were working mines and industries, joint-stock companies trading to the Persian Gulf, Canada, and the Baltic. Indeed, 1588, not 1688, is the deciding date for our purpose, for the modernizing of England proceeded much faster in the first than in the second century of the two before us, and the really creative work was finished before the Armada set out to destroy it. Once grant these conditions of Elizabethan England, and the decisions of the seventeenth century follow in natural sequence. No censorship could dam this current of free opinion, no paternal Government curb the desire for wealth, no King force a policy on this intelligent and solid ruling class, no one structure of society (however excellent) comprehend a community so various and modern. Both Strafford and Cromwell, then, were pulling against wind and tide; irresistibly the stream moves on to its appointed outlet—the placid, orderly, and final Revolution of 1688.

The exploits, material and spiritual, of these two centuries must always be dear to Englishmen. In their span parliamentary government was settled, the predominance of the Commons won, and the Cabinet system planted. The Anglican Church and Protestant dissent each proved too mighty to destroy the other. Ireland was, for the first time, firmly linked to Britain, and the way prepared for union with Scotland. The spur of gain, religion, or adventure, sent London merchants, Devon yeomen, or East Anglian Puritans to every corner of the earth, and the Empire was founded in America, India, and Africa. The royal navy and the regular army each had a glorious baptism of fire. A new literature burst out in sudden and astonishing magnificence. Finally, while Europe ran with bloodshed in the name of religion, or of Hapsburg, Valois, and Vasa, England completed in virtual peace her revolution from medieval to modern times, and made such strides towards modern levels of civil freedom, that even the next great turmoil of 1789 could be surmounted, with easy and legitimate developments from the constant principles of our government.

The generations who commanded this success also deserved it. In an age of personal government, our rulers were often supremely excellent, and rarely ignoble. One hundred and seven years were covered by the great names of Henry VII, Henry VIII, and Elizabeth. Both James I and Charles II, though stained by varying vices, had more than usual ability, and each stimulated some of the chief causes of future prosperity. The crime of Charles I lay in his method, not in his ideals, some of which were noble, and nobly defended even to the scaffold. Oliver Cromwell, a plain country gentleman, closed a civil war, united three kingdoms, and hoisted the English flag high in Europe. But the citizens were greater than their rulers, and all that is most goodly in our heritage is due to the astonishing talent and force of Englishmen between 1550 and 1688. In politics, Burghley and Walsingham,

Strafford and Pym, Vane and Ireton, Clarendon and Monk, Shaftesbury and Halifax. In
the Church, Cranmer, Parker, Jewel, Laud,
Andrewes, Jeremy Taylor, the seven bishops;
among the Dissenters, Cartwright, Penn, Baxter, Bunyan. For each name in literature, a
score of equal genius are omitted, and one
page of the mind can hardly contain Spenser
and Shakespeare, Marlowe and Jonson, Donne
and Marvell, Burton and Browne, Milton and
Dryden. In the high altitudes of thought
there are Hooker, Bacon, Selden, Hobbes,
Wren, and Locke; on the steep ground of
heroic action, or pure ideal, we may recall
Sidney, Drake, Frobisher, Blake, Eliot, Falkland. Stronger still is the impression of sane
ability and varied power to be gathered from
records of average lives. We find a middle
class ready to shoulder the burden of ad-
ministering a modern state—ardent, like the
Gilberts, to explore new continents—prepared,
like Blake, equally to command a navy or
defend a town. Raw recruits, trained by
Oliver's officers and put in red coats, defeat
Condé; fishermen cross the Atlantic in ten
or twenty-ton boats to fight the Spaniard,
or steer through icebergs to the promised
North-West Passage; women stand sieges
in manor-houses, boys the rack for their belief;

courtiers, weavers, old priests, meet the axe or enter the fire with a prayer for the State which thus tortures them. And the race which could furnish so many martyrs waged civil war with marvellous humanity, spent large sums upon charity and social welfare, and showed in the ordinary round of civil life an almost uniform moderation and good humour. True, there were faults, enough and to spare, in an age which at one end evoked the satire of More's *Utopia*, at the other the comedy of Congreve. It was superstitious, fiercely acquisitive, financially corrupt, unsparingly cruel to avowed enemies; men burned witches, imprisoned debtors and imbeciles in foul cells, oppressed their weaker neighbours, robbed the State, executed those who came within the remotest fringe of heresy or treason. But no age has been more crowded with personality and pure heroism.

In three vital respects it differed, even at its close, from our own. It was a rural age, and possession of land was the road to power. It was aristocratic, and gave short shrift to a theory or practice of equality. And it was an age of dogmatic religion; faith alone could move the large illiterate masses. Religion divided parties, coloured foreign policy, and gave a new fierce note to English patriotism :

" Verily," said Latimer, " He hath showed Himself the God of England."

Yet, taken all in all, few periods of history had better balance and poise. The aristocracy was not an eighteenth-century plutocracy, but still founded upon nature, service, and merit. The age is full of " new men " of the yeoman and shopkeeper class, who found fortunes and pass on higher; a great career was open to talent, and service to the State richly rewarded. Wealth was not unevenly distributed; the number of landowners still very large. Capitalism was a matter of many small masters; nor was the industrial fabric yet exposed to shocks from all quarters of the globe. England was not yet bisected into rural and industrial areas, industry was well distributed and linked to agriculture by a domestic system which made the peasant family half small holder, half industrialist. This balance, which obtained in society, seems to apply also to the national politics. The Reformation does not, as in some countries, cut every strand with the past ; it does not founder, as elsewhere, in bloodshed or anarchy. The strong arm of the Tudors saved much of the Church's Catholic tradition, and maintained, as against Protestant individualism, the strong machine of the State. In Church and State alike a *via media* was, by

1688, well established; Anglo-Catholic and Protestant, prerogative and individual liberty, order and progress, the best of both halves of the world-order which the sixteenth century had riven asunder, were preserved for the future. It is only after 1660 that we begin to be conscious that in one grave particular the balance threatens to break down—that the defence of the poor, which all Governments till that date had made their care, is exposed to growing danger.

The people, who carved out for themselves so deep a niche of glory, and for their posterity so great a fortune, were few in number and limited in resource. Forty millions, perhaps, in our values, was the utmost revenue that could be raised in 1688; the population of England and Wales, which in 1485 was about four millions, was even now not more than five and a half, or one million, perhaps, of men of fighting age.

II

THE END OF THE MIDDLE AGES—1485-1527

THE year 1485 in itself begins nothing save a new dynasty. Identical dangers troubled both the " old " and the " new " Monarchy—pretenders, nobles, social revolution. To crush them, Henry VII merely elaborated the Lancastrian Star Chamber and the Yorkist Council in the North, and imitated that reliance on the middle classes, who had served Edward IV so well. Parliaments were still few and far between; revenue was constantly raised by judicial extortion and benevolences. If Henry VII followed the peace policy of his Beaufort ancestors, Henry VIII, like the Yorkists, tried to conquer in France. The Church still carried her head high, and four great prelates—Morton, Fox, Warham, and Wolsey —held for forty years chief place in the Council. It is only with the Reformation Parliament that a real beginning is made of the Tudors' characteristic achievements, of a national Church, parliamentary monarchy, and

British policy; and the immediate difference between this dynasty and their predecessors was one not of measures, but men.

The two Kings were themselves chief architects of their success. The father, at his accession twenty-eight years old, had shown nerve and restraint in adversity; when fortune smiled, he was merciful, prompt, and industrious. His own memoranda prove his attention to detail, his curiosity in new things and human character, his continuous but not sordid economy. His lungs were weak, and neither his physical nor moral traits made for popularity, but he was a great ruler. No one better appreciated that English interests lay in peace and the balance of power. His legislation, drafted for the most part under his own eye, was solid and bold. Fourteen years' exile in France had given him a liking for French ways of government, and he showed with advancing age the same blend of avarice and superstition as Louis XI. His religion, and other good qualities, may well have come from his mother, Lady Margaret Beaufort, who was only fourteen years his senior, and had twice as much influence upon him as his beautiful, colourless wife, Elizabeth of York.

When Henry VIII succeeded in 1509, being not quite eighteen, scholars and ambassadors

vied in his praise. Nature and art made him
a royal manly figure—a mighty archer, jouster,
and tennis player. He was proficient in Latin,
French, and Italian, could compose an anthem,
amend a confession of faith, draft telling state-
papers, and reduce an audience to tears by
virile, high-coloured eloquence. When this
leonine figure grew to his full stature, he passed
in strength every beast of the field, and few
statesmen have shown greater capacity for
growth. He began by squandering his father's
treasure in reckless war and his own youth
in noisy dalliance; he lived to drive a great
mass of constructive policy through a doubting
people, foreign foes, and hairbreadth danger.
Of his vices more than enough must appear
hereafter; in early days, when in the Renaissance to be young and unopposed was very
heaven, they were barely suspected.

But the first task of these gifted Tudors
called for arts more primitive than popularity :
they had to avoid the fate of Richard III,
whose naked body, slung over a horse, was
carted away from Bosworth field. Sedition
and contempt for law had become a habit with
the nobility. The House of York had many
offspring and wide-stretching roots. Its brain
was Edward IV's sister Margaret, Duchess
dowager of Burgundy; its chance lay in the

discord of England, the sympathy of Yorkist
Ireland, and the wish of Scotland and Europe
to embarrass the new King. The military
leader of the first serious conspiracy was John
de la Pole, son of Margaret's sister, Lady
Suffolk. He was killed at Stoke, the battle
which disposed of their tool, Lambert Simnel;
but from Germany and the Netherlands his
brothers Edmund and Richard long maintained the feud. The first, handed over in
1506 by the Archduke Philip, was executed by
Henry VIII; Richard, "the White Rose,"
escaping all duns and assassins, died with the
French army at Pavia.

Far more dangerous to the Tudors was the
artistic plot which from 1492–99 circled round
Perkin Warbeck, a boatman's son from
Tournai. He, too, was exploited by Duchess
Margaret, and coached in the English language
and the rôle of Richard of York. Accepted for
a season as a prince at Paris and Vienna, he
once invaded England from Scotland with
James IV, and once from Ireland to join the
rebels of Cornwall. An effort to escape
brought him to the block in 1499, and he
dragged down with him Clarence's son, the
innocent Warwick.

The treason of William Stanley, brother of
the King's stepfather, Derby, proved the

incorrigible factiousness of the nobles, and Henry's reign did not close threats to the throne; to which, in the absence of heirs male, any descendant of Edward IV, or even of Edward III, could aspire. The Devon Courtenays, children of Edward IV's daughter Catharine, and Clarence's daughter, Lady Salisbury, with her children the Poles, waited for their doom till the stress of Reformation; but in 1521 the execution of Buckingham, in 1547 that of his grandson, the poet Surrey, showed again the crime of adding to other offences a strain of the blood royal.

Besides attacks on the King's title, armed resistance and riot filled these early years. Provinces remote from the capital were naturally pre-eminent. Yorkist propaganda and dislike of taxation accounted for the death in a skirmish of Northumberland, ruler of the North for the Crown. In 1497 the Cornishmen, refusing to pay a subsidy, marched without resistance on London, to be routed by Henry's strategy on Blackheath. Murderous assaults on foreigners and royal officials lasted throughout the time of Wolsey.

Royal policy cannot be held responsible for this ugly temper. An olive branch had been held out to the De la Poles, and in two ex-Yorkists, Surrey and Northumberland, Henry

VII found loyal servants. His marriage in 1486 to Edward's daughter Elizabeth had been planned during his exile to unite the Roses, and later measures showed his decided purpose to close revolutions. Landed title was protected by proof of five years' possession, and obedience to the King *de facto* ensured immunity from the treason law. The man who in 1485 had promptly compensated villages looted by his invading army was not likely to punish for punishment's sake, and leniency to the rank and file, ruthless penalties for the leaders, was the Tudor rule.

But lenity could not minister to this diseased nation ; nor was the fifteenth-century Parliament, elected at rare intervals under aristocratic pressure, the tonic required. The root evils were the Crown's poverty, and the defiant lawlessness of nobles as strong as the King. The remedies prescribed were those tried both by Lancaster and York ; to form the Council predominantly of commoners and to extend its powers, to destroy livery, maintenance, and riot, to resume royal grants, and build up a standing revenue. What was new was that, this time, the remedies were seriously and continuously applied.

Peerages were sparingly created, and Surrey

(or Norfolk as he became later) the only peer high in authority. The backbone of government were ecclesiastics like Morton and Wolsey, commoners like Poynings or More, royal servants like Empson, Dudley, and Pace. Great reliance was, it is true, put on individuals like Northumberland or Henry VIII's brother-in-law Brandon, duke of Suffolk, but none on the nobles as a caste. The decisive step of the first Tudor session was to swear the legislature against livery, forcible interference with justice, and all other offences which had made the nobles notorious; an act of 1487 gave to a special committee the statutory powers formerly exercised against the over-mighty subject by the Council, on its judicial side in the Star Chamber. Far from setting up a new court, or limiting the Council's authority, the act merely continued the efforts of previous sovereigns, and formed a first instalment of many measures for strengthening the main-spring of the Government. Thus another statute of 1504 anticipated the later division between the political council in attendance on the King and the judicial section in Star Chamber, and Henry VII continued the York-ist departments, which later blossomed into Councils for the North and the Marches, and the Court of Requests for hearing poor suitors.

The first requisite for dealing with the aristocracy was this reorganized Council, acting without a jury, examining on oath or secret information, and representing the King's person, for whom a chair was always set in Star Chamber. The second need was strong finance. Royal grants made since 1455 were therefore resumed and, together with the lands of Lancaster and York and others from attainder, swelled the domain revenue to £100,000. The customs, and tonnage and poundage were granted for life. Rich men had to give loans and benevolences, and if Empson and Dudley, the past masters of such methods, were executed by Henry VIII, it did not discourage others, for Wolsey's exactions were just as severe. By such means, coupled with a liberal use of vacant bishoprics and feudal dues, Henry VII was able in one year to pay out £90,000 from his privy purse, and to leave his son a great fortune.

A third essential for internal peace was the restoration of local government. Here the first Tudor essayed the task which all his family were to follow—the winning of the country gentry to the Crown. He subjected the magistrates to his judges, armed them with drastic powers against magnates and sheriffs, and stretched their commission to deal with new burning questions, like vagrancy or supervision of the guilds. The task was to be long: the men were still corrupt, but a beginning was made, and the swinging capital punishment, which More deplored in his *Utopia*, was necessary to exorcise anarchy.

But discipline alone could never pacify a nation; rather was it the impression that the King's government was giving them much of what they desired—peace, prosperity, and prestige. Social demands, to which the people's ballads testify, were met by legislation, not so much new in principle as carrying to firm conclusions the steps taken by the Yorkists to satisfy an aggressive changing society. Every decade that society, made up of substantial merchants trading overseas and large farmers cultivating for profit, grew more capitalistic in structure. Growth of national and international markets was followed by increasing definition, in theory and practice, of State control. Guilds working for local fairs, manors farming for their own needs, ceased to be the type; Cotswold wool passing in regular stream to Antwerp, Berkshire wheat down Thames to London, English consuls at Pisa or in Crete—such were the symptoms of

enlarged trade. Intense national rivalries
enhanced the need for a national system; the
mercantile ideal of England came in view—of a
teeming population, duly balanced between
industry and agriculture, as between con-
sumers and producers, not drained by foreign
imports or alien merchants, guarding its bullion, carrying in its own ships, mighty in its
men.

The weapons of this most political economy
were tariffs, subsidies, and safeguarding. An
Act of Henry VII's first parliament, one of a
long series of Navigation Acts, confined the
Bordeaux wine-trade to English bottoms.
Treaties were made with Denmark to get
access to Iceland fisheries, or with Riga to
reach Baltic naval stores. With Venice a
tariff war was waged, to capture the carrying
of Levant wines; another, less successful, to
break the Hanse merchants' monopoly of the
Prussian ports. Both Kings built royal war-
ships; Henry VIII fortified the Thames, and
founded Trinity House to perpetuate " the art
of mariners."

The Staple merchants, who still monopolized
the export of wool, were subsidized from the
Customs, that they might upkeep their mart at
Calais, but the cloth trade was more important
to national wealth. For this the Netherlands

were the vital market, and the ruin of English clothiers was the worst consequence of Burgundian patronage of Warbeck. Any political settlement with the Hapsburghs involved, therefore, making favourable provision for the Merchant Adventurers, and the delicacy of the interests at stake was seen in the friction arising out of the *Magnus Intercursus* of 1496, or the *Intercursus Malus* ten years later. Indeed, on the moot point of selling English cloth retail no satisfaction could be obtained. Commercially, England was still immature, as the power of the Hanse and other large alien colonies in London showed; the surest, though most troublesome, guarantee for future progress were those riots against foreign traders which taxed the efforts of the Tudor police.

The ramifications of the cloth trade, so sensitive abroad, necessitated close supervision at home. To balance it between Staple and Adventurers, or London and the provinces, was difficult, and its effects on agriculture menacing. Demand for raw material, demand for food, meant enclosure for pasture and for grain. The enclosing process, which had begun spontaneously a century before, now became ceaseless and high-handed; preambles of statutes, More and Colet, sermons and ballads, bewail the eviction of sturdy tillers and archers for shepherds and silly sheep, the pulling down of hamlets, the swift creation of a vagrant proletariate. A mass of legislation and royal commissions failed to check landowners pursuing a course which trebled their profits, but if clothiers' and farmers' riches were proved alike by Customs revenue, statistics of building, and educational charities a bitter legacy in the soil was left to the next generation.

Other industries called for like assistance. Capital and labour, both breaking out of guild restrictions, were migrating to suburbs or country, to find freedom, raw material, charcoal or water power. Protection, or fiscal privileges, were given to industries that claimed to be "infant," languishing, or essential—to London silk-weavers, Norwich worsted-makers, or Bridport rope-manufacturers. Towards the wage-earner the policy anticipated, in main lines, that of the next century. The sin of idleness was the stock theme of the legislature, and the lot of the vagrant who would not, or the unemployed who could not, find work, was made deliberately unhappy. Statutes fixed maximum wages, and long minimum hours; unemployed were forced to accept work at the legal rate, and breach of contract was punishable with imprisonment. On all sides Tudor law breathes the same conviction that, both for rich and poor, order was the first aim of society.

The previous century had proved the close connection of this order with peace abroad. Normally, English foreign policy continued medieval, until Reformation and oceanic-colonial rivalry brought in new motives; France was still " the ancient enemy " and trade with Flanders the ruling factor. What was new was the sudden competition of three great Powers in France, Spain, and the Empire, and the adjustment of this problem to England's vital interests. Peace was, doubtless, desirable for a new and shaky dynasty, but the conclusion that entire non-interference in Europe was the true policy, is as modern as it is facile. Popularity, if it does not condone a policy, explains it, and war with France was popular, not only with apprentices and ballad-singers, but with the martial classes. The Continent harboured many English rebels, and Scotland was the Continent's back-door. Nor was the ownership of the Channel and Atlantic ports immaterial, even in time of peace, for international law was in its barbarous infancy, and commercial jealousy

slid easily from tariffs to privateering. As for
the balance of power, the scales had never been
more heavily weighted, or more nicely poised,
and the isolation deemed magnificent in a
nineteenth-century Empire would have been
precarious in the age of Machiavelli. Seen in
this light, Henry VII's marriage projects, or
Wolsey's kaleidoscopic treaties, represent
what Bismarck called re-insurance, and had
more purpose than at first appears.

Henry VII's only war shows the value he
set upon peace. The occasion was the French
threat to Brittany,—last survivor of French
feudal fiefs, strong on the Channel, bound to
Henry by ties of his exile. It was only when
the war in a military sense was over, and when
the marriage of the Breton duchess Anne with
Charles VIII in 1491 destroyed its pretext, that
Henry took his army to France, and disclosed
the price he asked for a peace that he had no
purpose of refusing. By the treaty of Etaples
he obtained from France a large war indemnity,
and a pledge to harbour no English rebels.

He used this war not only to make peace pay,
but to win a lasting alliance with Spain, and
this friendship remained the kernel of his
system, as it did with his successors for nearly
a century. The treaty provided for the
marriage of Catharine of Aragon, daughter of

Ferdinand and Isabella, to Arthur, Prince of
Wales, and long before these children grew up
to be married, in 1501, the alliance proved its
worth. For fortune favoured the Tudors,
since in 1494 the long duel of France and Spain
began for the mastery of Italy. From 1496
the marriage of Ferdinand's daughter Joanna
to the Archduke Philip raised for France a
terrifying phantom of encirclement by a
Hapsburg–Spanish empire. Neutrality from
England, at the lowest, thus became a prize
worth winning; for this, Ferdinand would
close the Continent to Warbeck and save his
daughter's throne. His hand can be traced in
Henry's reconciliation with Warbeck's patrons,
in the *Magnus Intercursus,* and in the long-
drawn plans for Anglo-Scottish peace.

Henry's Scottish policy was inspired by no
vision of Union; merely by his usual cool
temporizing. For real peace with Scotland
was Utopian. The violent deaths of her Kings
made constancy impossible; her nobles could
be trusted for nothing but assassination, the
Border could be inflamed by a few pounds well
distributed. The Yorkists' capture of Berwick had deepened hatred for England, and
bitter experience was to prove that only
cordial relations with France could keep their
Scottish clients quiet. The marriage at last

accomplished between Henry's daughter Margaret and James IV was, then, rather an expedient than a project of empire, and served only for ten years to postpone this recurring war.

Yet opportunism constantly repeated becomes statesmanship of a secondary order, and the peaceful remnant of Henry's reign was as skilfully conducted as it was lucky. His weight in the balance was increased by the death of Isabella of Castile, which separated Ferdinand from the Hapsburghs. In 1502 Arthur—the next year his mother—died, and the hands of the two Henries came into the market. Historians have seen a decay, mental and moral, in the intrigues respecting Catharine's *dot*, or inquiries for the King's remarriage with the twice-widowed Margaret, Regent of the Netherlands, or with the lunatic Joanna of Spain; the conclusion does not seem to be called for. The future of Europe, especially of Spain, was entirely uncertain. It were wise, then, to retain the possibility of Catharine's remarriage to Prince Henry, or to clinch it by Papal dispensation, but politic also to show, as by the Prince's signed protest against it, that England need not hurry her decision. If Spain collapsed, good relations with the Regent Margaret were essential; the

c

retail cloth trade, assigned to England by
treaty, was the background to this elderly
romance. Best of all was the sequel in the
marriage by proxy (December 1508) of the
King's daughter Mary to the Archduke
Charles, heir prospective to Austria, Spain, and
Burgundy. Till that was achieved, the hap-
less Catharine might be kept on short commons, and Ferdinand be left suspended over
his abyss in Castile.

Far different was the early policy of Henry
VIII, marked as it is by two wars and restless,
gorgeous diplomacy. The King (so proud of
his legs) bestrode the stage as mediator, de-
fender of the faith, and potential Emperor;
Wolsey, as far greater than any Pope. Of
those who have judged this policy sterile or
extravagant, some have cleared the King at the
expense of the Cardinal, others the converse.
It is, indeed, hardly possible to overdraw the
influence in this period of Wolsey, the grazier's
son, risen by way of an Oxford fellowship and
Bishop Fox's favour to be Chancellor, Papal
legate, and chief minister. The King was in
his first popular beauty: it was hard to get
at him amid jousting and junketing, music
and reading. Business was therefore piled on
the Cardinal, who in Star Chamber reproved
the gentry and checked enclosure, in Chancery

and the Requests heard poor suitors, in Council prepared every detail of war and negotiation, in Parliament had to justify taxes and defend the Church. Yet Henry's early masterfulness in other branches is well established; his ambition to shine in Europe was coupled with personal jealousy of Francis I, and years after Wolsey's fall he engaged again in French warfare. The first of the series (1511–13) was due in part to an orthodox desire to defend a Pope menaced by French schism, in part to that wish for popularity which made him execute his father's agents, and again to promptings from Ferdinand and the Emperor Maximilian, each (in James I's phrase) "an old and experienced King." The Queen's influence (for so Catharine had become in accordance with Henry VII's last wishes) was naturally used to cement the Spanish alliance.

Prestige, nearly ruined in 1512, was restored in full measure the next year—in the Battle of the Spurs, the capture of Tournai, the destruction of the Scots and their King at Flodden. From this date till the second French war of 1521 a peace, armed and feverish, obtained in Europe.

Death swept off the old players. Louis XII made way for the more dangerous Francis, Ferdinand for the Archduke Charles, Maximilian in 1519 for the same. At each stroke new uncertainty, new alliances. Wolsey's policy, avowed to foreign envoys and English councillors, was to keep the balance, to prevent the union of two powers against England, and ensure a share in all profits. Twice he countered the junction of the Hapsburgs with France by outbidding them at Paris : in 1514 marrying Henry's sister Mary to Louis XII, in 1518 pledging his daughter Mary to the Dauphin and selling Tournai back to France. But the election of Charles V to the Empire, making war between him and Francis certain, set a new and decisive test for this hitherto not inglorious English diplomacy. A modern eye could find a dozen reasons for non-intervention—in the state of the Church, of Ireland, or of the very balance of Europe. One common explanation, that Wolsey wanted Charles' assistance to be Pope, is ruled out by the logic of dates ; history must, it seems, be content with the common popularity of the war, with the commercial value of Charles' friendship, with Henry's wish to pull his weight, and his sympathy with the Emperor, like himself the opponent of Luther. For in 1521 the royal author produced his Defence of the Sacraments.

The war's military fruits were insignificant;

invasion from Scotland was repulsed, but two raids into France were indecisive. In 1525 Charles crushed the French at Pavia, and Francis went to Madrid as a prisoner. Indefatigably, Wolsey set about redressing the balance which England had helped to overturn; again Mary's hand was pledged to a French prince and the Pope encouraged to resist Imperial aggression. But early in 1527 questions arose which threatened to destroy the Cardinal's symmetrical diplomacy. Henry's projected divorce would illegitimize Mary, the destined bride of France; it would, moreover, embarrass the Pope, whose capital was sacked in May by the Imperialists, and whose person was soon at the Emperor's mercy. Not only so; stormy scenes in Council and Parliament menaced the national accord, which for a generation the Tudors had maintained.

The friendly public opinion on which these despots without an army depended, was not expressed by parliamentary government. Six parliaments did, indeed, meet from 1485-97, but their sessions were brief, and one only was held between the last date and 1509. The next three sessions up to 1515 did little but grant war taxes, while from 1515 to 1523, as again from 1524-29, Parliament was not summoned at all.

In fact, the Constitution in our sense, with
fixed functions and binding rules, did not
exist. The King's two capacities—the one
personal, the other public—were still blended.
The private revenues of Lancaster or York
were pooled with public grants, and administered through the Wardrobe, the Household
treasury. Some ministers—Lord Steward or
Lord Chamberlain—were half personal servants, and the personal secretary was not yet
transmuted into a Secretary of State. With
the King lay the sole initiative, and he could
exert it through different sections of his councillors. Parliament sat in the palace of Westminster, the home of the King and his Household, and the "Parliament chamber," which
saw the rare meetings of his great council of
Parliament, could also witness ceremonial
ablutions of Knights of the Bath. Laws might
solemnly be declared in Parliament, but were
commonly drafted by the judges who advised
the Council in Star Chamber. Royal action
was limited rather by usage than by statute,
and moved on various levels of constitutional
consent. Thus, arrears of a benevolence were
ordered to be collected by authority of a
statute; a great council in 1495 pledged Parliament to taxes in advance; Henry VII was
empowered by statute to repeal attainders.
Soldiers were still levied by commissions of

array, by orders to " defend the coasts," or by
indentures with powerful subjects. Loans or
gifts taken on progress formed a fair part of
the revenue; as late as 1525 Wolsey asked a
benevolence of one-sixth from the laity, and
one-fourth from the clergy.

But the general resistance in this last case
shows the fallacy of thinking that the early
Tudors were reckoned above the law. Even
in 1485 we read of resistance to attainder,
while the subsidy given for life was to form
no precedent. The Commons of 1523 made
ominously clear the limits to obedience. For
four months they hotly contested the Budget,
asking Wolsey to withdraw from their presence.
Every measure affecting the life, property, or
industry of large classes, was passed in the form
of statutes. Parliament required increasing
control from above, and successive royal agents
—Lovell, Empson, Dudley, and More—were
made Speakers for this purpose.

Indeed, one becomes conscious, as Henry
VIII's reign wears on, that some angel is
stirring the waters, that acquiescence in strong
government, to escape anarchy, is yielding to
more or less vocal opposition. More's acclamation at the accession of a young idealist King
is succeeded in 1516 by printed criticism in the
Utopia, portraying to a restless age the extravagance of war, the laxity of the Church,

and the wretchedness of the poor. Already
the Commons in 1515 had betrayed their
anxiety to attack Bishops and Church courts.
The work of Colet, Dean of St. Paul's, founder
of that school and interpreter of the Apostle,
was sufficiently done; the Universities were
resounding with the feud of the new Grecians
and old " Trojans." The printing press was
directing a stream of critical knowledge on to
all things established. The earliest editions
of printed Statutes appeared under the first
Tudor " despot; " in 1520 an Oxford book-
seller sold over 2000 printed books; already
a " Christian Brotherhood " in London were
distributing imported New Testaments. The
old earth was passing away. Cabot's voyages
from Bristol had brought news of strange
western isles, Vasco da Gama had rounded the
Cape, Eastern products were unsettling the
Continental Bourses. Rome, mistress of the
old world, was in 1527 ravaged by Lutheran
mercenaries, the new barbarians.

As for England, the throne lacked an heir
male; the King's Highness was beset by unsuccessful war, internal disorder, and trouble
domestic. The classes and interests, which
the Tudors had set out to satisfy, were once
more tossing to and fro. It was time for new
remedies, and for the Middle Ages to end.

CHAPTER III

HENRY VIII AND THE REFORMATION

THE last twenty years of Henry VIII form one of the irrevocable periods in English history; the foundations then laid still hold up modern society. The Church was violently torn from the Roman communion and jurisdiction. A new aristocracy replaced the monasteries. The English Bible created Puritanism, and sowed grain for democracy. Parliament at last became a familiar branch of government. Wales and Marches were reduced to something like uniformity with the standards of London. Ireland was at length subdued.

It is possible to be grateful for this solid achievement, without admiring its agents. The last half of Henry's reign is the very definition of tyranny, and the methods of his Reformation were sordid and inhuman. Over the whole process sprawls the great bulk of the King, changing every day further from that gracious Renaissance prince, who had talked philosophy with More at Chelsea, and charmed all hearts by his gay vitality. No minister replaced Wolsey in concentrated power, and Henry's self-will extemporised its own law. From the inner chambers of his nature—strange compound of political insight, moral scruple, and animal desire—slowly unrolled that narrow *via media* along which all England must march. Deviation meant death to those who, " faint to God, faint to the truth, faint to His Highness," found some different clue to the maze of conscience and policy, or developed reservations of their own. Thomas More, though willing to obey a *de facto* succession, perished for silent disapproval of Henry's second marriage. Lack of beauty and political assets in Anne of Cleves doomed Cromwell. It became treason to express doubt of Henry's religious supremacy, treason for an unchaste woman to wed the Supreme Head. Catholics, who repudiated the succession, died alongside Lutherans who denied transubstantiation.

A murderous cynicism contaminated King and Court. Henry rejoiced in public at Catharine's death, and betrothed Jane Seymour on the morrow of Anne Boleyn's execution. Catharine Howard privately rehearsed her own tragedy, block and all. Abbots

were denounced and dragged to gibbets by
their neighbours. Many individuals grew
rich, but morals and religion poor indeed.
And the moral tone, like every stage of this
first reformation, was determined from the
Court. No spontaneous enthusiasm can be
traced in Parliament or people; the crime,
as well as the achievement, is pre-eminently
the King's. His hand's cunning in politics
grew with experience and sole command, and
the nation, less cowed than dumbfounded or
corrupted, genuinely admired him. Against
a black background we must set hard facts;
that through such tribulation the whole
Reformation world had to pass, that the
bloodshed and destruction abroad were ten
times more severe, that, if suffering and
martyrdom were the seed, the final harvest
was individual liberty and constitutional
government.

This end was far, indeed, from the thoughts
of Henry and his subjects, when in 1527 the
Divorce first troubled Wolsey's peace; far
from the cardinal's servant, Thomas Cromwell, whose will, drafted in these years,
bequeathed his soul to the Virgin and legacies
to London Franciscans. The Divorce project, originally unconnected with religion,
sprang from a mixture of passion and policy.

Catharine's marriage, repellent to many from
the first, had failed in all its objects. Of six
children, only the eleven-year-old Mary survived, and the Spanish alliance by 1527 was
broken down. Henry had long been unfaith-
ful, and his illegitimate son, the boy Rich-
mond, might provide one solution. But in
1520 Norfolk's nieces, the Boleyn sisters,
caught the royal eye; Mary was for some
years the reigning mistress, to be replaced
about 1526 by Anne, whom, by the date of
the sack of Rome, Henry was determined to
marry. He cherished hopes of this reward
for his services to the Holy See; he could
point to dispensations given for his sister
Mary's marriage to Suffolk, and for his sister
Margaret's divorce from Angus, her second
husband.

Two years were enough to dispel this
dream. What was asked of Clement VII
was considerable : to obliterate the solemn
dispensation granted for Catharine's remarriage by Julius II, and to overlook the notorious
intimacy of Henry with the elder Boleyn.
If a Medici Pope could get over such matters
of principle, the military situation made him,
for practical purposes, an Imperial prisoner,
and if in the scant days of French military
success he could toy with notions of bigamy

for Henry, or a nunnery for Catharine, hard
facts in the end kept him true to his office.
For Catharine was unyielding, and in June
1529 the treaty of Cambrai put Italy and
Papacy in the Emperor's hands. The commission to try the divorce, which had been
committed to Wolsey and Cardinal Cam-
peggio, was revoked in July, and in October
Wolsey fell.

To him the divorce was sheer fatality. It
destroyed the marriage planned between Mary
and Orleans, as part of the French alliance;
Anne Boleyn's candidature demolished his
second plan of a French match for Henry;
her hatred, with that of the Howards, poisoned
Henry's mind. Desperately Wolsey lent himself to forward a scheme he had not approved,
menaced Rome with schism, searched Cam-
peggio's baggage for lacking documents, en-
treated France to save Clement in his own
despite. Failure to meet Henry's wishes was
unforgivable; fallen so low, Wolsey turned
to duties long neglected and aspirations long
cherished, visited his York diocese, and pushed
on his Oxford college. His enemies would
never have left him at peace; as it was, the
wish to recover power led him into dangerous
correspondence, and when in November 1530
he died at Leicester, he was going under

escort to the Tower. He had made England eminent, and given her domestic peace, but now he was useless; for Henry at the close of 1529 summoned Parliament, to redress " the enormities of the clergy."

In a campaign directed to forcing Rome into surrender, Henry could reckon on strong support. To large sections the Church officials and monks were detestable; in London, and in the coast shires trading with Europe, this anti-clericalism was rabid. Colet and the Renaissance leaders had firmly underlined the worldliness of prelates, and the slothful superstition of monks. Lollardy had never been extinguished, and the burning of a few heretics, and of many heretic books, continued till Lutheran literature was smuggled into London.

For this criticism of the Church there was ample warrant, for all the evils which had convulsed Germany flourished in England. There were too many clergy; the towns were full of young priests demoralised by freedom from duty save singing of chantry masses. They were deeply secularized, from absentee political bishops down to household chaplains, who kept the farm accounts or brewed the ale. Exemptions and laxity had ruined discipline. The moral standard was low;

the Cardinal had his illegitimate children,
the Abbot of St. Albans his mistress, the
grossness of priests and friars garnished
quarter sessions. Monasticism was decayed.
Few houses had been founded in the last
century; many were half empty, many
financially straitened. Some principal abbeys
had won hatred as enclosers, some smaller
ones were living in flagrant vice.

Two grievances touched the King and
nation more nearly. The Church courts'
power over clerks, or " benefit of clergy,"
had been cut down by recent legislation, but
in 1515 a clerical effort was made to rescind
the statute which deprived of such privilege
murderers and robbers in minor orders.
Wolsey tried to refer the question to Rome,
but King, judges, and Parliament showed
their teeth. Henry declared that he, like all
English kings, had no earthly superior; the
judges spoke of *praemunire ;* Parliament was
quickly dissolved. Even more irritating and
persistent was Church jurisdiction over laymen in cases of probate, testament, tithe,
libel, and other offences which, under the
vague heading of morals, the clergy had con-
trived to keep from the common law. The
fees of these courts were large, their methods
inquisitorial, while behind them was the

appeal court at Rome. But to this hard
and competitive age the money grievance
most appealed. The clergy's endowed wealth
was great, but they exacted vast additional
sums from the people. Some went to Rome
in annates (the first year's income of a benefice),
Peter's pence, patronage for Italians, and
judicial fees; but more to the Church at
home. "The parson sheareth," wrote Tyndale, the translator of the New Testament,
"the parish priest polleth, the friar scrapeth,
and the pardoner pareth; we lack but a
butcher to pull off the skin." For this they
had not long to wait.

The memorable seven years of the Reformation Parliament divide at 1533, which marks
the marriage of Henry with Anne, the breach
with Rome, and the beginning of seven years
of terror. Was the verdict of Parliament
that of a free body? The Commons were
"packed," in the sense that all sixteenth-
century Commons were packed; a large
number of royal servants had found seats,
provided by direct pressure in the few constituencies which the Crown could influence,
but far more by indirect pressure through the
landowners, who returned most members.
The Crown, as always, took the initiative;
thus the Commons' "Supplication against

the clergy " was drafted in Cromwell's circle. Members' readiness to attack the money abuses need not be doubted; their wish to change the fabric, question the faith, or depart from Rome, is much more arguable. In 1529 Henry had to interrogate one committee in Star Chamber; in 1532 these curious reformers begged to be dissolved; the great Acts against annates and appeals were both opposed. In secular matters they contested Henry's wishes more ardently; they showed their dislike of making words constitute treason, and twice threw out the Statute of Uses which impaired their freedom of settling lands on whom they willed. But no politician save More, no bishop save Fisher of Rochester, was found to refuse the royal supremacy, and no member of the Commons suffered for his faith. The legislature were incited by appeals to national prejudice and private gain; as a body, most of them were ready to follow Henry's rearrangements of the succession; as individuals (and not least strong Catholics like Norfolk) they swallowed monastic lands. They would not initiate an attack on the Church, but neither would they defend it; only in this Laodicean sense can Henry's Reformation be described as a national revolt.

He entrusted the management of this cold

D

Parliament and this reluctant Church to two new advisers. The theological amenity and literary grace of Thomas Cranmer deeply impressed the succeeding twenty years. From a chaplaincy with the Boleyns and foreign embassies, he was chosen to follow Warham at Canterbury in 1532, and alone among leading councillors kept Henry's favour to the end. He was married to the niece of a German reformer, and was the first Englishman to view reform of the English Church as part of a great movement. He kept close contact with Reformers in all Europe, and adapted their liturgies to his own perfect English. In no servile sense, but as the vane exposed to the elements of heaven, he vibrated to every current in the intellectual air. If Cranmer imparted this faint spiritual glory to the Reformation, Thomas Cromwell personified its force, and only the austerest historical canon could refuse him greatness. A self-made man, by his wits he built up a fortune as merchant and solicitor, transacted business for Wolsey but opposed his costly foreign policy, and at his fall swiftly found new patrons. His experience was worldly, his mind material and entirely modern. He was the earliest of those " Italianate " Englishmen whom contemporaries thought the devil incarnate, owned books like Petrarch, and quoted Machiavelli. His knowledge of northern Europe was limited, and his foreign policy insular. He was corrupt and obsequious to the King, but had a notion of " the commonwealth " which resembled an ideal. Dogmatic religion meant little or nothing to him, and if in time he moved, faster than Henry liked, towards Protestantism, it was because the fire of hostility to the new State was kindled by Catholics. Like the greatest of his name, he was a man of action, and to him must be ascribed the parliamentary pressure, the ruthlessness, and the redoubled speed, of Reformation after 1533.

All done until that date was tentative, or preparatory. Neither the appeal to the universities of Europe, nor the Act against annates, involved a final breach. Legislation was pushed forward to whet the appetites of the laity and to intimidate the Church. In the session of 1529–30 statutes passed to fix fees, to limit pluralism, to check clergy engaging in trade. In 1531 the bludgeon of *Praemunire*, that had crushed Wolsey, descended on Convocation, which was made to recognize Henry as supreme Head, " so far as the law of Christ allows." In 1532 he

forced the clergy to accept three articles that
meant total surrender; canons were henceforth to be made only with royal licence and
approval, and a commission was to revise
ecclesiastical law.

In spite of such blows at the clergy,
embassies to the Pope at Bologna or to
Catharine at Dunstable, in spite of the orthodoxy Henry proved by excluding Lutheran
books, the doors he wished to open remained
shut; if the promised heir to the throne was
to be legitimate, he must break them down.
His secret marriage to Anne in January 1533
was the first step towards what must end in
open revolution. In February an Act was
passed, forbidding appeals to Rome; in April
Cranmer declared void Henry's first marriage;
in September Elizabeth, eldest daughter of
the Reformation, was born. Against foreign
intervention Henry was assured by warfare
between France and the Empire, and the
year 1534 clinched all that had gone before.
Annates were transferred to the Crown, all
money payments cut off, the election of
bishops made solely dependent on royal
licence. The Act of Succession vested the
inheritance in Anne's children; all subjects
could be asked to admit that the first marriage
had been invalid, and that the Pope had

violated the law of God. The Treason Act
attached direst penalties to words, maliciously
spoken, against the title or orthodoxy of the
sovereign.

Catholic resistance, beginning even before
Henry's new edifice was completed, in the
oracles of the Nun of Kent found and exploited
a channel for the general detestation of the
King's marriage. The execution of this
hysterical peasant and her accomplices did
not seriously test Henry's resolve to drive
the whole realm along his chosen road; but
those of 1535 horrified England and Europe.
It was a new outrage that Carthusian monks
should be beheaded in their robes; how much
more amazing the execution of Fisher, a
bishop and Cardinal, and of More, ex-Chancel-
lor and most famous of living Englishmen!
Though neither would accept the Supremacy
or the Succession oath, More had done nothing overt against them, while Fisher, though
in touch with Spain, was old and dying.
But Henry's effort to incriminate them earlier,
his refusal to accept a jot of compromise, and
the scandalous means used to secure their
condemnation, show that he meant to spare
none, however eminent or moderate. The
issue was, in fact, come down to fundamentals; it was, as More declared, " against

one realm the consent of all Christendom for more than a thousand years." Henry had transformed the Church-state into an Erastian State-church, but in so doing he had changed the emphasis, not the substance of society. For a belief in the unity of the realm, in the junction of Church and State, and the sin of toleration, was common to all parties; those who had scattered Wycliffe's ashes and burned Hus had no logical ground for grievance. It is this which gives an inevitability to all Henry's proceedings; " by the law of the State," as many of his victims resignedly confessed, " they were justly to die."

The enforcement of this newly modelled, but old-principled, unity was committed in January 1535 to Cromwell as vicar-general, and six months later he began a visitation of the monasteries. In his mind this purpose had, no doubt, long existed. He had promised to make his master the richest king in Europe; the threatened vengeance of Catholic kings meant expensive armaments, and the Crown's fixed revenues were declining with the value of money. The monasteries' landed income was some £140,000, their lands perhaps an eighth of the cultivated area. Precedents for secularization or readjustment were plentiful. Henry V had reformed the Benedictines and dissolved alien priories, Waynflete and Wolsey had broken up monasteries to form their colleges. The case for reform was equally strong. The monastic ideal was perishing; benefaction had long been flowing in other channels. One episcopal visitation after another had condemned grave immorality on paper, and condoned it by trivial punishment. In one sense, too, the road towards secularization had long been opened, for many houses had leased land to neighbouring gentry, who by acting as stewards, advocates, or recipients of corrodies, had acquired some vested interest in the estate.

Cromwell's visitation was no honest inquiry, but a search for material to justify a preconceived sentence; the low type of adventurers who were visitors did not see more than one-third of the houses, and inspected those they saw at the rate of twenty a fortnight. But the Act of 1536 was moderate, in deference perhaps either to Cranmer and Latimer, who hoped to reform the monasteries into places of education, or to the squires, who in several cases opposed suppression. Dissolution was, for the moment, confined to houses with less than £200 a year, and they were some 350 in number.

The majority fell later, though by no

legislative process, for the Act of 1539 merely
consecrated the facts. Their fall was part
of the Crown's policy after 1537, consequent
on the revelation of Catholic conspiracy on a
European scale. The abbots of some, like
Fountains or Glastonbury, were attainted;
some had sold their goods, and could not pay
their way; most could not pass the tight
mesh of Cromwell's Injunctions. These and
other iniquities added about 250 houses, and
those the greatest, to the total. Some seven
thousand monks and nuns were thrown into
the jostling lay world; their tenants and
dependants had to make what terms they
could with new landlords, or swell the population of loafers in the towns. An orgy of
loot—of land, lead, jewels, bells, and fish-
ponds—in which courtiers, squires, and villagers
combined, desolated the sites once filled with
holiness and learning; in the rare habitations
of the medieval mitred abbots, a new English
aristocracy cheerfully laid the foundations of
enduring homes. The money received by
Henry's Court of Augmentations was larger
than supposed, but his plans for re-edifying
the Church dwindled down to six new bishoprics. To the Church the dissolution was
more positively disastrous, for the money
spent by monasteries on education now dried

up, and the new landlords took over their appropriated parish tithe. The rate of ordination dropped, ignorance and poverty dogged the Church till Laud's day, and the desert was filled by the advent of the Puritans.

Hitherto, Henry's Reformation had been purely destructive, but he was to find that his purpose of reforming without change of faith was an illusion. The first recognition of this came in the Ten Articles, the Bishops' book explaining them, and Cromwell's Injunctions. The Lutheranism of these documents was only an aroma: the Real Presence was still asserted, the seven sacraments retained, even images condemned only for abuse, and a delicate equilibrium kept between faith and good works. But the spark of dogmatic change was struck by orders for printing the English Bible, and for teaching Articles, Creed, and Commandments, to the people in their own tongue. Henry in person (all in white satin) could prove his orthodoxy by a death sentence on John Lambert for denying a Real Presence, but Lambert at the stake, crying "None but Christ," represented the future.

The fury of doctrine was to haunt Henry's last years, and all those of his children; his immediate task was to crush the last resistance of the Catholic world. It broke out first in the Pilgrimage of Grace; in order of time, as in moral dignity, the northern peasants preceded Catholic nobles and European Powers. These Lincolnshire and Yorkshire rebels were not revolutionary, but fanatically conservative. They felt, as Norfolk felt who was sent to defeat them, that " it was never merry since the new learning came up." They asked restoration of the monasteries, dismissal of Cranmer, Cromwell, and the reforming bishops, repeal of Succession and Treason Acts, destruction of Tyndale's Bible, prevention of enclosure, freedom of elections, and a Parliament at York. Spreading from Lincoln across the Humber, the revolt enveloped the whole North, and half by fear, half willingly, swept nobles and gentry into a rising sprung from the masses. Their banner of the five Sacred Wounds covered the cause of the Catholic feudal North, against a heretic and centralizing State. But the last popular protest was also the noblest, for no democratic movement was ever less stained by crime, and Aske, the Yorkshire barrister who led it, was the purest figure of the age.

In 1537 Aske, Lord Darcy, and the abbot of Fountains, went with hundreds more to execution, and the new State survived its

greatest trial. Henry never faltered in his
purpose of repression, but never was the
Tudor star of good luck so resplendent.
Paul III's effort to make peace between the
Emperor and Francis was slow to succeed;
his cardinal legate, Reginald Pole, was kept
at arm's length by the rivals, each of whom
hoped for English support or neutrality. It
was only in the middle of 1538 that peace
was achieved in Europe, only in December
that Henry was excommunicated. Even
then Catholic union proved an empty menace;
Catharine of Aragon's death relieved her
nephew Charles of an awkward obligation,
Flemish commerce required peace with
England, Turks and Lutherans occupied him
on two sides. To the fulminations of Pole,
the threats of invasion, and the linking up
of English Catholicism with Europe, Ireland,
and the Scots, Henry replied by destroying
the old nobility, especially any whose claims
could endanger his throne, and the grandsons
of Edward IV and Clarence suffered for their
blend of royal blood with lost causes. By
1540 the King stood triumphant. The birth
of Edward VI (1537), which had killed his
mother Jane Seymour, gave a new life to the
dynasty.

But warnings of trouble, within and with-

out, had been sharp, and Henry, like all
Tudors, reacted promptly to opinion. He
delighted in popularity, but the Reformation, as personified in Cromwell, was loathed.
He gloried in order; the new Bible preachers
were upsetting society. His own orthodoxy
was unshaken, and Catholicism in England
was the first condition of non-intervention
from abroad. The Six Articles of 1539 represent his own policy of reaction, and were
vindicated in the Lords by his own royal
mouth. They made denial of transubstantiation a heresy, and reaffirmed clerical celibacy,
private masses, and confession. Their popularity proves that he had well gauged the
average mind, the deprivation of Latimer for
resisting them, that the fight of old and new
creeds was really beginning.

But no submission could save Cromwell
from Catholic hatred, and, luckily for them,
he himself repeated in 1540 all those circumstances which had ruined Wolsey. Once
more a minister, hated by the rest of the
Council, embarrassed both the King's matri-
monial relations and his scheme of foreign
affairs. The marriage with Anne of Cleves
was not the first time that Cromwell had
pressed German alliances. The Duke of
Cleves, in politics (though not in faith) a

Lutheran, was the arch-enemy of Charles V, and brother-in-law to the Saxon elector. Nothing but fear of a combined attack could have induced Henry to sign the treaty; within a few months he found himself married to a plain and uncultivated woman (who had hurriedly to be taught cards at Calais), and expected to shield her brother from the Emperor. The execution of Cromwell and the dissolution of this marriage were Henry's further steps to recover the *via media :* till the end of the reign his great ability was devoted to its maintenance. The " King's Book " of 1543 expounded the position of the Six Articles; the reading of the Bible was continued, but only for the propertied classes; the King's last will and testament itself halts between Catholic and Protestant language. In him the new unity seemed incarnate, and not over England only, but over a United Kingdom, that great shadow was spreading.

For the Reformation created the State by a concentration of powers. Disunity, which had hitherto been a passing phase or inevitable weakness, now became a matter of dear life; if a lukewarm bishop or a disloyal justice were dangerous, how much more a lawless Palatine or an enemy neighbouring kingdom. It is this which gives a certain

grandeur to Cromwell's machinations, or to
Henry's bellicose decision that the whole
realm must march together. One by one
the old franchises were absorbed. An Act
of 1536 vested in the Crown the palatinate
courts of Durham, and Cheshire was given
representation in Parliament. The statute
of 1535, in finishing the anachronism of the
Welsh Marches, completed the work of the
Yorkist Council set up at Ludlow. Not
Catholicism but anarchy was here the danger,
and the Council of the Marches, under the
resolute bishop Lee, mingled Erastianism and
execution in due proportion.

Ireland was to prove a much more lasting
difficulty, but here also Cromwell was the
first minister to grasp the nettle. The conquest advocated by Norfolk, Henry's first
Deputy, had been abandoned on grounds of
expense, with the result of allowing the
House of Kildare to oppress its rivals and
create a chaos. Reformation made conquest
a necessity. Irish emissaries began their
long connection with England's enemies, and
the seizure and execution of Kildare in 1535
was followed by the extension to Ireland of
the Supreme Headship in all its details.
This period of blood and iron was succeeded
in 1541 by a lull in which the reign closed;
a slow policy of Anglicanizing and civilizing

Irish chieftains was tried as an alternative
to war.

If this left it uncertain whether Catholicism
and racial pride would fuse in a solid mass
against England, this unhappy result followed
in Scotland as a direct consequence of Henry's
aggression. The system of subsidizing a
Scottish baronial faction, pursued by all the
Tudors, inclined the Scottish King to France.
Scottish Catholicism was gross but powerful,
and had in Cardinal Beaton a resolute leader.
James V's two French marriages were concluded against his uncle Henry's expressed
wishes, and the war against France in 1544
was chiefly aimed at her ally. The capture
of Boulogne was spectacular, but Henry
hoped vainly to involve Charles and Francis
in a wasting war, while he disposed of Scotland. As it was, he could only patch up a
truce with France, and meantime alienated
Scotland for a generation by making the
marriage of their Princess Mary with his son
the condition of peace, and by sending
Hertford to waste Lothian and Edinburgh.

The last phase of Henry's policy was therefore aggressive, incomplete, and costly. The
forced loans of 1544-5 were severe; debase-
ment of the currency set a ruinous precedent,
and redoubled the general wretchedness.
Yet never had the King's prestige with his

people been so undoubted. Unitedly they rallied to resist any threatened invasion. Parliament gave him power to settle the Crown by will, and a free hand over heresy by proclamation. The Commons, packed by Cromwell, attainted their creator and allowed Henry to imprison their Speaker. Convocation with scandalous servility dissolved the marriage with Anne of Cleves. Norfolk, most powerful and accommodating of servants, at Henry's death was awaiting the execution already meted out to Surrey, his brilliant son.

This despotism, real as it was, was yet, as Raleigh said of Elizabeth's, " not Turklike "; it was, rather, Cæsarism of genius, Buonopartism minus the army. By force of character, corruption, prestige, and terror, Henry created and courted the chameleon termed public opinion. He brought every marriage and doctrine to the bar of Parliament; there he reorganized his Household, set up his Court of Wards, and affirmed the powers of his various councils. By making the Commons act for forty years under his eye, he branded on a whole generation the majesty, unity, and empire of the State. But Phaeton could not ride unscathed the sun's chariot, and Henry by calling on opinion, even that of a restricted Parliament, was asking a whirlwind to escort his safe, prudential reformation. The criticism he invited against Rome rent his own Council; the country was divided by two sects of extremists. In vain, agonizing with his ulcered leg, did he plead for unity, and deplore the wrangling of " that precious jewel, the Word of God," in every ale-house. Who but he had brought the Word down to the ale-house, or opened in Parliament the *arcana* of government?

No such reign as this, which closed with Henry's death in January 1547, had been seen since that of the first Edward. Edward had made government national, Henry by fusing Church and State made it omnipotent. With due allowance for times and seasons, their method was much the same; that all cards should be laid on the table made no difference to the rigour of their game. Henry, like Edward, was by instinct a despot, and like him left a country crippled by bad finance and beset by contradictions of policy.

St. Peter, says an old biographer of the Borgias, was told not to despise things unclean. It is hardly for Englishmen, who have inherited parliamentary liberties and Protestantism, to try in the scales the political genius and the monstrous iniquity of Henry VIII.

E

CHAPTER IV

THE DECIDING YEARS, 1547–61

THE blackest periods in English history appear to coincide with the maximum influence of foreign theories and foreign politicians. Edward VI and Mary reigned in such an age; German and Italian theology was followed by a ruinous stretch of Spanish power, and only Elizabeth restored the conservative insularity of her father's reformation.

There were good reasons for the darkness of Edward's reign. Sir Thomas Smith, one of Somerset's few friends and later Secretary to Elizabeth, insists in his account of the constitution that "the Prince is the life, the head, and the authority of all things that be done in the realm of England." But in 1547 Edward was only nine years old, and, precocious though his mind was, a sovereign who died at fifteen was necessarily ruled by others. The passions, therefore, which the strong Henry had restrained, found a vent, and England was carried towards civil war by two factions, keyed up by doctrinal

66

hatreds, anxious for power, hungry to exploit the quick profit which business men could make of " reformation." To survive in politics meant connivance; to win, almost necessitated crime. Treachery, timidity, and greed in various degrees marked the origin of the political houses—Howards, Russells, Herberts, or Cecils—who now set out to make or mar. Somerset, the sole idealist among them, was moral only in compartments, and his politics show a distasteful mixture of Somerset House and Exeter Hall. John Dudley, son of Henry VII's agent and father of Elizabeth's favourite Leicester, became under his new title of Northumberland the most daring criminal of the century.

But the best of governments would have been severely tested, for the sum total of human misery in England from 1540–70 defied speedy remedies. Part, no question, was directly due to bad administration. Henry VIII left one-fifth of alloy in his gold currency, and two-thirds in his silver; Northumberland raised the last proportion to three-quarters, and called the shilling down to sixpence. A ruinous policy of loans and inordinate speculation redoubled disturbance of prices. But the sharpest change of price levels in British history was mainly caused by economic motives that were worldwide—revolutionary dislocation of markets and trade-routes, importations of bullion, and collapse of the medieval structure of industry. Profits, enclosures, and rents accelerated, but wages lagged behind. The Act of 1547, that destroyed the religious endowment of the guilds, removed another prop of the poor man's independence, as well as some funds for popular education; persistent fraud vitiated commerce. Worst of all was the harsh temper, which Latimer reproached in the Protestant laity. Resistance to Somerset's benevolent autocracy was intelligible, but the legislators treated Edward's proposals with the same contumely. They fixed penalties of treason on those who resisted enclosure, of felony on those who combined to lower prices, and literally branded the vagabond as " an enemy to the commonwealth."

The gap between the old order and the new was filled with the social misery and panic that accompanies revolutions. Woe to London, cried the preachers, the new Nineveh, where Christ and the poor lay uncared-for in the streets. Evangelical democracy raised its head, as it had in Germany; pamphlets advanced the rights of all for whom Christ had died.

Henry VIII's choice of councillors and tutors for his son marked a decision for further Protestant advance, but Somerset, the Protector chosen by the Council, allowed advance in a shape the King would have detested. The wish expressed by Parliament for "a lighter garment" was natural after the strain of the last ten years, but the repeal of Henry's heresy and treason laws *in toto*, of the Act of Proclamations and the Six Articles, gave radical reform a strong start, which the legislation of 1549 never caught up, and the absence of law left room for a popular, extra-legal, religious anarchy.

The mob dipped their handkerchiefs in Somerset's blood on the scaffold and treasured his memory, for his sympathy with the oppressed and his dreams of liberty were sincere. But the social reformer must either be Cæsar, or above suspicion; he, on the contrary, depended on a fluctuating Council, and criticism could find a dozen weak points in his armour. He took Maiden Bradley and much monastic wealth, built Somerset House from proceeds of churches and chantries, and set up an illegal court. A stigma, natural if unjustified, attached to him for the execution of his brother, Thomas Seymour, a villain who aspired to the hand of Princess

Elizabeth, dabbled in piracy, and conspired against the State.

Armed with little but good intentions, the Protector had to meet forces which demanded the strength and prestige of a Cromwell. His religious settlement followed the lines indicated by Henry, and later approved by Elizabeth. Abolition of clerical celibacy, grant of communion in two kinds, and services in English, prepared the way for the Act of Uniformity and Prayer book of 1549. From this the Catholics in Parliament were strong enough to exclude Cranmer's drastic reform of the Sacrament, and the Real Presence was retained. No compulsion to uniformity was put upon laymen, and the Princess Mary was allowed her Mass.

But Somerset's aspirations for religious peace were soon thwarted. The Catholic leader, Bishop Gardiner of Winchester, refused all compromise and was imprisoned. Rebellion in Cornwall and Devon (January to September, 1549) demanded restoration of the Mass and the Six Articles, and recall of Cardinal Pole. On the other side, a torrent of foreign teachers, illustrious and obscure, poured out the full Protestant programme in London and the Universities. The pure faith, suppressed by Charles V

abroad, sought refuge in England, which for
ten years was whirled round in the diurnal
course of the European Reformation. The
Pole, John a Lasco, was laying hands on
godly elders in Austin Friars, Italian Peter
Martyr was in command at Oxford, German
Bucer at Cambridge, a Strasburg congregation in the holy valley of Glastonbury. One
may reasonably doubt the lasting influence of
Stumphius or Unterhovius upon Anglicanism,
but at the time it was profound, and militant
Protestants took orders not from Canterbury
or Whitehall, but from the masterful Popes
of Zurich and Geneva.

East Anglian Protestantism of this sort
laid its foundations in 1549 in social revolution. Somerset's sympathy with victims of
enclosure was notorious, and the commission
he issued to check it had for its leading spirit
John Hales, who had vainly sought a remedy
from Parliament. The gentry offered a solid
passive resistance to the commissioners, and
the whole South was disturbed by agrarian
trouble; in Norfolk, under the rich yeoman
Ket, the peasants captured Norwich and
routed one royal army.

While the Western rebels had no social
demand but limitation of gentlemen's servants,
the Easterners hoped to abolish private

property. But both risings were quickly suppressed; not by Somerset, but by his rivals Northumberland and Russell, not wholly by English troops, but German and Italian mercenaries.

These English divisions, which Somerset was unable or unwilling to mend, were enough to dispose of his foreign policy. By defeating the Scots at Pinkie, he seemed at first to have crowned Henry's campaigns, and he spoke ardently of a union of hearts between the Kingdoms. But force only revived Scottish patriotism; their young Queen Mary was hurried to France, and under cover of the English troubles Henry II laid siege to Boulogne. The fall of Somerset at the end of 1549 was the certain result of his virtues and his weakness, and it was enforced by men of both religions; his execution two years later was brought about by Northumberland alone, whose path to power was barred by Somerset's popularity and scruples. So did weak good intentions make their invariable room for crime.

Northumberland's first exploit was an ignominious peace with France, by which England surrendered Boulogne and abandoned hopes of directing Scotland. Representing no popular interest, for no man had

punished rebels more severely, and no religious
sincerity, for this Protestant politician swore
on the scaffold to his Catholicism, he had
no chance of backing, financial or otherwise,
from a Parliament, the meeting of which he
postponed till his greatest design made it
inevitable. But money he must have to
content his faction, and money was best
forthcoming by posing as the Moses of Reformation. He proceeded, then, to break up
the Catholic group who had helped him
against Somerset; Bishops Gardiner, Bonner,
and Tunstall were deprived, the crafty Paget
disgraced, and Mary's household scattered.
The spoils oozed out to the ruling clique;
the bishoprics of Durham and Gloucester
were " suppressed," church plate seized, and
chantry lands sold. Meanwhile the Church
was tumbling into ruins. New bishops like
Hooper or Ridley refused to admit a Real
Presence or wear the surplice, altars were
turned into tables, scandals over clerical
marriages and clerical ignorance demoralized
many parishes. Foreign immigrants were
only united in disobeying the law, and every
heresy that had cursed the first four centuries
of Christendom afflicted the country from
which Henry VIII had banned " diversity
of opinions."

The second " settlement " of the reign was duly signalized in 1552 by a second Prayer-book and Act of Uniformity.   This time it was root and branch.   The vestments authorized in 1549 were abolished; the altar dwindled to a table; the negation of a Real Presence was emphasized by a special rubric, added at the instance of John Knox, one of North-umberland's bishops-designate.   Cranmer's essentially un-catholic mind embarked on a reformation of Canon law, which contem-plated a semi-presbyterian scheme of synods : a third offence against the Act of Uniformity was made punishable with life imprisonment. Passive resistance to this violence, and fierce debates in Parliament, showed the prob-ability of reaction, which was assured by national misery and Northumberland's crimes. On the first, it is enough to say that, while millions of money were paid out to the Duke's followers, all that was done for the masses was the organization of cavalry to repress them.

And now, for the first of two occasions in this period, the most powerful politician in England manufactured a scheme to alter the legal succession.   But Shaftesbury's Exclu-sion Bill of 1680 was venial compared with Northumberland's project, which involved

intimidation of Parliament and forgery of
the King's hand. Edward's remaining papers
prove that he could recognize his subjects'
sufferings, but in him, as in Mary, religious
bigotry blinded a strong sense. On this
chord Northumberland had played, but harp
he never so wisely, he could not keep alive a
consumptive King. Hence the desperate plot
to win the Crown for one of the Protestant
Greys, granddaughters of Henry VIII's sister,
the Duchess of Suffolk, who were postponed
by his will to Mary and Elizabeth; hence
the marriage of Guilford Dudley to Lady
Jane Grey, the student of Plato and all things
of good report, innocent victim, in her sixteenth year, of the Reformation at its vilest.
The King's death demolished a scheme which
demanded repudiation of Henry's will, of an
Act of Parliament, of two heirs, and which
Council and judges had only accepted under
force. The aristocracy, so long excluded
from power, asserted themselves, and in
three weeks saved hereditary monarchy.
Edward died on the 6th July; on the 3rd
August Mary entered London in triumph.
The last Catholic reaction had begun.

For Catholic to some extent it was. Sir
Thomas Wyatt raised the Protestant standard
in Kent, but the Londoners' apathy and

Mary's courage settled the issue. The reversal of Edward's Church legislation created no difficulty, and ten of his bishops continued in office. But one year was long enough to show that the restored Catholicism was that of Henry VIII, not Henry VII. If two-thirds at least of Mary's parish priests later accepted Elizabeth's settlement, their Catholicism was clearly more Anglican than Papal. The veteran advisers now readmitted to Council—Norfolk, Gardiner, or Paget—had, after all, accepted Henry's breach with Rome. The Queen's second Parliament refused to disinherit Elizabeth; lay peers, led by Paget, rejected a bill to revive heresy laws; a third Parliament, which made this concession, was careful (packed though it was) to protect holders of monastic estates by terrors of *praemunire*. Yorkshire might still be Catholic, but London, the centre of government and trade, was vociferously Protestant.

Mary's easy accession, then, though in part a protest against Reformation in advance of public opinion, was much more reaction against sordid adventurers and bad government, the act of a people loyal to hereditary succession and conservative in change. In this view experienced politicians of all schools agreed, and the Spaniards, who in their own states persecuted relentlessly, urged moderation on the English Queen.

But Mary, who might have won a fair hearing for her faith in a favourable atmosphere, ruined her popularity by marrying the Spaniard Philip. Loyalty to the memory of her Spanish mother, devotion to the Church she had never abandoned, and reverence for her cousin the Emperor, were rooted in her, and now at the age of thirty-seven, worn and embittered by harsh treatment at Protestant hands, to these loyalties she dedicated her life. The marriage was her own device; both Gardiner and Pole opposed it. National pride, maritime jealousy, and religious fears, made common cause; her first Parliament had asked her to marry an Englishman, and when her marriage, hedged about by many legislative safeguards, was accomplished, men's eyes turned to young Courtenay of Devon, or to Elizabeth.

Its effects justified these forebodings. Philip's efforts to make Englishmen swallow Spanish pensions, and himself swallow English beer, did not mellow the situation. To his fury, Parliament declined to crown him, and he revenged himself on Mary by absence and infidelity. The son, for whom all was prepared, never came to console her, and, lastly,

Spain dragged her into war with France and
conflict with Rome. Pope Paul IV's ven-
detta against Philip and Pole left England
cold; not so, the neglect of English interests
in Scotland, commercial opposition from
Flanders, forced loans, base coinage, and in
January 1558 the inglorious loss of Calais.
England was a victim to Hapsburg-Valois
rivalry; behind the conspiracies of Wyatt,
Courtenay, and Stafford, Henry II and his
alert envoy Noailles were pushing French
penetration and the pretensions of Mary,
Queen of Scots.

If Mary made national resistance probable
by accepting Spanish dictation in politics,
she ensured it by ignoring Spanish advice in
religion. The packed Parliament of 1554
restored the Lancastrian heresy laws and
repealed the whole anti-Papal legislation of
Henry VIII. Reginald Pole, the twenty
years' exile, was brought back to preside, as
legate and archbishop, over the revival of
the old cause, for which his family had died.
Though a liberal by Roman standards, he
was bent on suppressing heresy, and to him
and the Queen personally—not to Spain, nor
to Gardiner, who died in 1555—responsibility
must be given for the burnings.

Measured by Spanish examples the number

was small, about 300 in less than four years, but the *auto da fe* had not been seen in England on that scale, and all evidence shows the execration they evoked. The victims, generally, were drawn from two classes: the leading Protestant divines who had not fled into exile, and humble villagers, including sixty women. Of the total over one-third came from Bonner's diocese of London; Lincoln and East Anglia had many, the North and the West not ten between them. The two Englands, that asked such different forms of government and were so often to fight again in rival camps, were now divided by religion.

Four leaders of Edwardian Protestantism —Cranmer, Latimer, Hooper and Ridley— headed this army of martyrs, but neither this, nor the faster rate of execution as the reign went on, produced any genuine Catholic revival. The middle of the century was a close time for English religion and political energy; the exile of many active spirits, the connivance of others at practices they disliked, dulled resistance in Parliament and aspiration in literature. Bowing in the house of Rimmon, the nation sullenly waited for the Queen's death. It came, and Pole's also, on the 17th November, 1558; a week later

Elizabeth came to London from Hatfield, with
Cecil, its future owner, in command.

Her reign was to last forty-five years;
Cecil was for forty to be chief minister;
but their decisive measures were taken
within eighteen months, and Queen and
minister were never greater. The crisis was
immediate. Tortuous negotiations at Cateau
Cambrésis were ending the French war, but
a worse thing might come out of them than
the final loss of Calais—a Franco-Spanish
alliance. Within a few months Henry II's
death made Mary Queen of Scots, Queen of
France also, with a weak husband dominated
by her Guise uncles. Her gallant mother,
Mary of Guise, held out against Protestant
rebels in Edinburgh, and the Catholic north
of England was counting on Franco-Scottish
invasion. Any religious decision would involve risk; the wrong one would mean
rebellion. The Catholics were solid in the
Bishops' bench, the Peers, and the Council.
Mary had left a large debt and an empty
treasury; 14 per cent. was being paid on
loans at Antwerp; the forces were mutinous,
the ordnance non-existent.

To gain time to breathe was the first
necessity for this sick commonwealth; but
the endless vacillations, that Cecil's game
implied, blind us to the cold decision of these

first years. "Protestant" in some sense, the new settlement was bound to be. Elizabeth's sympathies had been undisguised during Mary's reign; the Papal cause was bound up with Spanish alliance, misery, and humiliation. The new Queen was decided to model her policy on her father's, the survivors of whose Council, conservative though they were, like Petre or Arundel, had fully accepted royal supremacy. Her inclinations were promptly shown in the use of English and a mangled Mass in her chapel, but hesitation was banished by the sentiments of the Commons elected in January 1559, who proposed to revive the title of Supreme Head, the second Prayer-book, and second Act of Uniformity. The lines of doctrine, blurred under Henry VIII, were hardening; if most of the Commons were really Protestant, the mass of the bishops and peerage were as staunchly Catholic. Bills for Supremacy and Uniformity were opposed in the Lords, and Convocation would not hear of compromise, while the need of humouring Catholic Europe was at least as great as that of reassuring Catholic England. The Government therefore decided to ask for less than the Commons desired.

By the Act of Supremacy Elizabeth took the less provocative title of Supreme Governor,

F

and admitted Convocation's right of assent
to definition of heresy. Her Act of Uniformity, while restoring Edward's second Prayer-
book, amended it in a manner that made it
at most Lutheran, and conceivably Catholic.
The Real Presence was not repudiated, and
might be read into the Communion; the
clerical dress was to be as in Edward's second
year. Royal Injunctions did, indeed, impugn
superstitious practices, but they subjected
clerical marriage to the bishops' license and
contradicted the Puritan idea of the Sabbath.
The Church was, then, put on a basis which
could be represented as not un-Catholic, and
as merely continuing Henry's system. Yet
in essence the new settlement was revolutionary. Save for a small body of official
divines, the clergy's chosen representatives
opposed it, and had no share in making the
Prayer-book. One only of Mary's bishops
continued, and twenty-five sees had to be
filled in 1559–60.

This settlement of English religion was
directly connected with foreign policy; for
the equilibrium of opinion, which enabled
Elizabeth to balance Catholic and reformer,
was matched by that external equilibrium
between France and Spain, which was to
give her thirty years of immunity from
serious war. The lasting conditions of English

success were already present; none the less,
the decision to be taken was a grave one.
By the Peace of Cateau Cambrésis France
kept Calais, and to this the English were
resigned. It was from the captor of Calais
that danger threatened, and the Duke of
Guise and his house reached their full ascendancy in July 1559, on the death of Henry II.
But in this very spring the national, religious,
and class feelings of the Scottish nobles
flared up against a French Catholic despotism,
and the Lords of the Congregation, with John
Knox beside them, appealed to the English
Government.

With cautious audacity Elizabeth and Cecil,
disregarding most of the Council, determined
to take this chance of evicting France from
Britain and of crippling the Catholic claimant
to England. They saw that they could
make Philip politically Protestant, for he
would give up many Masses rather than see
the French master Edinburgh. Screened by
the same fear on Philip's part, they had been
able to make their religious settlement in
security. Elizabeth courteously declined
Philip's hand and disregarded his envoy's
religious pleadings, but humoured him by
the amount of Catholicism she retained, or
suggestions of her marriage with a Hapsburg. The imperial votaress would even

confide her longing for a nunnery or, by
lighting an extra candle on her chapel altar,
rouse joy at Madrid over the sinner that
repented. It was Philip, then, who begged
Rome to withhold her excommunication, and
resignedly accepted the advice of his ministers,
that the one fatal disaster would be a French
victory in Scotland.

But Catholic states were not only dis-
united; they were, as Cecil discovered, limited
in resource. Civil war was breaking out in
France, while Philip had left rebellious Netherlands to find a troubled Mediterranean. Step
by step, adjusting religion at London to the
last news from Huguenot Normandy or dis-
contented Brussels, Elizabeth took the plunge
of helping the Scots' Protestant rebellion.
First money; then Winter's fleet in the
Forth; last, an army over the Border. Mary
of Guise, abandoned to her fate, died in
June 1560, and on July 6th the Treaty of
Edinburgh rewarded political courage. The
French troops left Scotland; the nobles,
bound to England by alliance, obtained a
share in the regency that waited the arrival
of their Queen.

Best of all, from Elizabeth's point of view,
was the inexpensiveness of her triumph, and
the restoration of national finance was the
third department, in which prompt action

stabilized the future. The issue of debased silver was stopped, its value called down by proclamation. In 1560 Government called in the whole mass minted since 1543, and in the space of a year completed the operation of a new issue. Strict economy, re-grant of first-fruits to the Crown, and a good deal of land-grabbing at the Church's expense, reduced the deficit. The coinage controversy had justified "Gresham's law," and Gresham himself was employed to deal with foreign manipulation of the exchanges. By good management and confidence, the interest on Government loans was reduced to 10 per cent., the total debt dropping from £279,000 in 1560 to £17,000 five years after.

Thanks, then, to the Providence whom the deist Elizabeth ever acknowledged, whose chief agent hitherto was the reluctant King of Spain, the Elizabethan Government won its respite for consolidation. No bloodshed had yet stained this revolution, and the impunity of Bonner and Paget is the clearest condemnation of Henry VIII's barbarity. Such peace was too good to last. Elizabeth was unmarried, and her health in these days uncertain. In August 1561 Mary Queen of Scots, the face that was to launch a thousand ships, crossed from France and reached Holyrood

CHAPTER V

THE ELIZABETHAN AGE

ROUND everything great in history arises an aura of legend often as potent as the original. As with Magna Carta or Napoleon, so it was with Elizabeth. The Virgin Queen, surrounded by Burghley and Sidney, Drake and Raleigh, the Gloriana of the poets, the hammer of Spaniard and Rome, is stamped irretrievably on the English mind, and raised in history, like the throne, above party. To her all the next century appealed. To restore the national equilibrium, that she maintained, was the ideal of Clarendon and Bolingbroke. The Protector invoked her when he re-opened war with Spain—" Queen Elizabeth of happy memory, we need not be ashamed to call her so." Bacon and Coke, apprenticed in her reign, handed on to the next the twin traditions of State and Common Law; Hobbes perpetuates her association of sovereign and people in one body politic. The Church, in Hooker's person, admitted in her its second

founder; " by the grace of God and His
servant Elizabeth we are." In any case,
neither facts nor legend give countenance to
that view of her reign which would substitute
economic mechanism for human will.

But the least " Elizabethan " figure of the
age was Elizabeth, who distrusted enthusiasm and poured cold douches of caution and
economy on her men of action. The great
achievements, or institutions, for which she
is famous, were wrought in her despite, save
only the Anglican Church, which in its pre-
Reformation type, its reservations, and its
political temperament, incorporates more of
her attitude to life than either democracy or
Empire.

Opportunism, which was her second nature,
became for her country a saving merit. Dogmatic pronouncements on religion, her marriage, or the succession, might plainly have
caused civil war; premature alliance with
Huguenots or Dutch would have precipitated
invasion. History cannot pronounce de-
cisively on problems the secret of which defied
Cecil and Walsingham. It is plausible to
assume that she had no religion and never
meant to marry, that she was incapable alike
of spiritual leanings, or of bearing children;
it is more important that she used these

mysteries with unfailing insight, baffling both
Europe and England by secret diplomacy or
brazen flirtation. Her strictly political gifts
were a curious blend between those of Henry
VII and Henry VIII. The parsimony of the
first in her ran riot. Her relations with Scotland and Holland were ever endangered by
it; even in the Armada year she was selling
muskets to her ill-paid soldiers. She had
Henry VIII's royal way with people and
Parliament—girding them to loyal passion,
silencing their dearest wishes with the Crown's
majesty, anon retreating in a cloud of sonor-
ous concession. She shared, too, his royal
temper, and would fly into tantrums over an
unfavourable despatch, or beer she did not
like, or the marriage of her favourite. As with
him, her affections embarrassed without
ruling policy. To the whims or graces of
Leicester or Essex she would mortgage Cabinet
harmony, revenues, reputation, but not power,
and if Machiavelli's test be sound, to judge the
sovereign by the ministers, she ranks high.

Nothing is more indicative of her settled
purpose than the immediate choice of Cecil to
manage the State, and Parker the Church.
Like herself, both had kept silence in Mary's
time; both were moderate, slow-moving, and
incorrupt. Cecil, long ago Somerset's secre-

tary and since manager of Elizabeth's private
finances, belonged to that English school of
politiques—Selden, Clarendon, Halifax, and
Harley—who have done most for the continuous life of the nation. His policy, habits,
and tastes, were all substantial and safe. He
was interested in landed property, shared in
industrial combines, studied genealogy and
family history. Trade seemed to him the
country's life-blood, and a settled reason
against war. He was less insular than his
countrymen, and far more Protestant than
his mistress, but in all things recognized that
accommodation is the salt of politics. He
dealt with problems as they arose, deducing
from the innumerable pros and cons, which
sprinkle his huge correspondence, a reasoned
path of safety.

The Archbishop had been Anne Boleyn's
chaplain and Bucer's friend, and save for his
marriage was all that Elizabeth could desire.
His learning was great, and the learned world's
debt to him lasting, for he saved from ob-
livion the old English Chronicles. His theological " mediocrity " was sincere, and he
supported unswervingly the royal policy of
comprehension. He shared, too, his mistress's conviction that a political menace was
implicit in democratic Protestantism.

Two factions endangered the Cecilian position. The one, which disappeared with the crisis of 1569–71, came from the Catholic and feudal influences represented by Norfolk, Westmoreland, and the surviving magnates. More constant was the personal factor of the favourites, Robert Dudley, Earl of Leicester, and his stepson Robert Devereux, Earl of Essex. But scandals like the death of Amy Robsart damaged Leicester, while Essex's popularity shipwrecked on military failure and insane egoism. From 1571, when Cecil became Lord Burghley, he and after him his son Robert, a handy pocket edition of his father, retained in fair security the substance of power.

Elizabeth's Council must be judged as a whole, and Anne Boleyn's daughter formed the heart of it from the bourgeois Protestant aristocracy whom she represented, particularly from her kinsfolk among them. Hunsdon, Mary Boleyn's son, was Lord Chamberlain and the warden of the Border; his brother-in-law, Knollys, had great authority; Walsingham, Secretary from 1573–90, was stepson to another Carey; the Admiral, Howard of Effingham, husband to a third; Walsingham's brother-in-law Mildmay, Chancellor of the Exchequer; another cousin of

the Boleyns, the cultivated Buckhurst, succeeded Burghley as Treasurer. No prelate sat
in this body of new talent, and no peer of
pre-Tudor creation : was not Burghley the
grandson of a yeoman in Henry VII's Chamber? Among other leaders, Sadler served
Elizabeth in Scotland as he had Henry VIII;
Smith, who followed Cecil as Secretary, had
been the same to Somerset; Crofts (like the
Careys) had conspired against Mary. Add that
Walsingham, Knollys, and Mildmay were
Puritans, and it is plain that Elizabeth knew
the true basis of her throne.

The bitter factions that distracted this
Council were not merely due to lust for power,
or the immorality which smirched the Virgin's
court. They fed, rather, on the baffling inter-
mixture of three problems, each enough to
test any ability and patriotism—the succession, religion, and foreign affairs. All three
met in Mary Queen of Scots, behind whom
might at any moment be ranged Scottish
nationality, English Catholicism, and the
whole fury of the Counter Reformation,
directed from Rome, Paris, and Madrid.
Providence, human frailty, and statesmanship, were to decree that these four corners of
the world never came upon England simultaneously, and this knowledge makes us

unjust to Elizabeth. The certainty that
Spain and France would not trust each other
to settle England upon Mary, the inevitability of war, the Armada's revelation of the
clouts that stuffed the Spanish colossus—
from these spring impatient surprise that,
years earlier, the Queen did not follow the
road pointed by the Protestant war party,
take up the cause of Christ against Belial,
combine Puritans, Dutch and Huguenots in a
holy war, and execute Mary, daughter of the
Amalekites.

The Queen's miserliness or her hatred of
assisting rebel Calvinists did, doubtless, assist
to postpone much that in modern eyes glorifies
her reign, but solid reasons for delay were overwhelming. To recognize a successor in 1560
or 1570 would have been her winding-sheet,
for neither Council, Parliament, nor people
were agreed. The Commons of these years
vociferated in favour of Catherine Grey, Lady
Jane's sister. But Henry VIII's will, that
supported Greys against Stuarts, was itself
questioned; Catherine's secret marriage to
Somerset's son Hertford discredited her; and
her death in 1568 left the field clear for Mary,
candidate of aristocratic England. Catholic
differences were buried in Mary's marriage
with her cousin Darnley, and the birth of

James I in 1566 provided the heir longed for by patriots in both kingdoms.

The murder of Darnley, the Bothwell scandal, Mary's eviction from Scotland and her arrival as an English prisoner, did not eliminate her claim, nor diminish the danger. Elizabeth herself long wavered; definite breach with Mary might jeopardize all that slow use of time would solve. The reaction, which might have been predicted from the Elizabethan settlement, flamed out at Mary's presence, and from 1569 Elizabeth and Cecil were fighting the majority in Council, Catholic and Protestant, who hoped to overthrow the chief minister, the Reformation, and the new State, through the marriage of Mary to Norfolk. That year the Catholic North, resentful of its lost faith and franchises, of *parvenus* in office, moneyed men, and strong government, pushed Northumberland and Westmoreland, the Northern earls, into rebellion. In 1570, too late to save the earls from defeat and exile, or the North from punitive executions, Pius V excommunicated the Queen as a Calvinist, inviting her subjects and Europe to depose her. The Ridolfi plot of 1571 revealed the willingness of Spain and Mary to obey this summons, even by assassination, and the treason of half the English Council. Norfolk,

their stalking horse, died next year on the
block; well might Elizabeth dally with
warrants and reprieves, for the execution
signalized a break with old England and the
elimination of Mary from the succession. It
stirred, too, the wave of anti-Catholic legislation which rose later to such savage detail,
and accounted by 1603 for the death of hard
on two hundred priests and laymen. Catholicism for three generations became identified
with treason, and Elizabeth, not of her own
volition, was placed at the head of Protestant
Europe.

But religion never determined Elizabethan
policy, and her change of alliances was accomplished by slow degrees. Having burned her
fingers in one religious enterprise, the aid sent
to the Huguenots in 1563, she realized that
only the French Government could assist her
in serious war with Spain. But against that
war both economy and the vital Flanders
trade, which took eighty per cent. of English
cloth, protested, while French politics offered
no guaranteed support. Catholic victory in
the religious wars of France seemed likely
after St. Bartholomew's, in 1572, or Henry
III's military ambition might give much
more help than Philip to a captive queen-
dowager of France; the Government of to-

day might vanish in some new turn of the kaleidoscope, as Catherine de Medici struggled to retain power and her son's affection.

Nor did the revolution against Spain in the Netherlands from 1567 afford an easy field for intervention. Annexation of harbours in Zealand would cost much money. Alva, and Parma after him, were great generals with trained armies. To join France in a Netherlands war, as Coligni suggested in 1570 and Anjou in 1580, might mean a worse thing than Spain: the French in occupation of Antwerp, "a pistol pointed at the heart of England." Finally, open war would rouse the Catholic conspirators crushed in 1571, and tempt the factions surrounding young James to rescue his mother.

The policy adopted, therefore, was to make war on the big scale unlikely by erecting it, on a small indirect scale, into a system; to fill the fire so full with irons that conflagration would be impossible. Treasure on its way to Philip was seized at Southampton, the Devon gentlemen pirates were let loose on the Spanish Main, the Dutch subsidized (but never to excess). The *Politique* section of French nobles were flattered by the marriage prospects dangled before Anjou, the heir, and stimulated in their historical antagonism to

Spain.   Scotland was kept in leash by maintaining alliance with the Protestant chieftains;
when Moray was assassinated, Morton was
patronized as regent; when French influence
threatened in 1582, the Raid of Ruthven
" rescued " the young king.   The Huguenots
received arms, money, volunteers, but not
alliance.   The German Calvinists were urged
to save true religion in France.   The Palatine
princes were brought to the Low Countries
to bridle the French.   Till something turned
up, Mary was to be kept alive; her death
would force a door which sooner or later would
be unlocked from inside.

A game of playing for time, that won
twenty years, cannot be called unsuccessful.
The real criticism is that Elizabeth prolonged
it after hope of accommodation had vanished;
so long, as to lose some of her potential allies;
so long, indeed, that her envoys went to meet
Parma, while the Armada was running up
the North Sea.   But only a rapid series of
unexpected changes justified the war policy
of Walsingham.

In 1580 Philip's conquest of Portugal
doubled his Atlantic sea-board and his colonies.
In 1584 Anjou died, Henry of Navarre, a
heretic, was heir to the French crown, the
Guises turned towards Spain.   The same year

William of Orange was murdered, and Parma carried faster the Spanish reconquest of the Low Countries, which Don John of Austria had begun. Despairing of help from France or her own son, Mary from prison implored it of Philip, to whom she made over her interest in the English crown. Most of all, the long-pent-up passions of churches and peoples broke from the control of governments. Seminary priests and Jesuits invaded England by scores. The saintly Campion, and many more, died for a faith which Rome had made synonymous with treason. Mendoza, Spanish ambassador at London, handled the threads which, passing through the hands of English exiles like Cardinal Allen or Parsons, began at Rome or Madrid, and ended in Mary's prison. Throgmorton's plot, endless assassination plots, drove Parliament in 1585 to form the Association that pledged them to avenge the Queen's death, and to exclude from the throne any in whose interest such crimes were committed; the mere presence of priests in England became punishable as treason. The Spanish-assisted raid upon Ireland in 1579 ended in a cold-blooded massacre of prisoners, a return for the recorded and unrecorded sufferings of English sailors in Inquisition cells. While the military situa-

G

tion in Europe stirred Elizabeth to decision, Drake's mastery of the Atlantic was doing the like with Philip; English seamen were severing the golden arteries which enlivened the huge body of Spain.

England first took the steps that forced on collision. In 1585 Leicester was sent to Holland with an army. In 1586 the Babington conspiracy was brought home by Walsingham to Mary; in February 1587 her head, so long demanded by the English Commons, fell on the block. Having failed in an attempt to instigate Mary's murder, Elizabeth failed likewise to delay Spanish action by disgracing the secretary who had signed the fatal warrant. Diplomatic expedients were played out and, delayed but not disabled by Drake's " singeing of his beard " at Cadiz, in June 1588 Philip sent the Armada.

The great test came, and England survived, thanks not so much to the Protestant winds, as to an overwhelming English superiority in seamanship, guns, and ships. But annihilation of one Spanish fleet did not end the war, which dragged on till 1604—a weary phase of petty expeditions and starved resources, showing Elizabeth unchanged and incorrigible. The well-conceived blows against the Azores and Cadiz, the help sent to Hol-

land, Normandy, and Brittany, were impaired
by faction, niggardliness, and vacillation, and
the heroic action of individuals, like Norris or
the fighting Veres, did less to defeat Philip
than Dutch nationality under Maurice of
Nassau, or the doggedness of Henry of
Navarre. By 1596 Leicester, Walsingham,
Drake, and Frobisher were dead, Essex as
leader of the sea-war party was spirited but
reckless, and Ireland began to drain English
strength.

The struggle of Reformation and Counter-
Reformation made Elizabethan policy not only
English but British, not insular but oceanic.
The infant ally, whom Henry VIII had half-
consciously nourished in Scottish Protestantism, was now full-grown, and made the best
safeguard against recurrence of the Catholic
grouping which in Mary's first years nearly
ruined England. Catholic or aristocratic
reaction was able to murder one regent in
Moray, to kill another, Lennox, in battle, to
bring a third, Morton, to the block, but two
things, more lasting than crime, every year
eased the strain. The one was Scottish
Presbyterianism, the other a real desire of
political leaders in both countries for James'
peaceful succession. The very fact that James
and Presbyterianism did not agree improved

the situation in English eyes, and made James more anxious not to risk a throne that would compensate for present humiliation. He might ask, then, the punishment of Spenser for poetic license against Mary, but offered only a bald protest at her execution; filial affection (which, after all, was hardly called for) was less potent than an English pension and a guarantee of the succession. The first was grudgingly granted him; the refusal of the second explains his intrigues in all quarters —with Spain, Rome, or Essex—but essentially he depended on the good will of Protestant England, and before 1603 was on clear terms with Robert Cecil. Scotland was thus at last detached from the Continent; at last peace reigned on the Border.

But between England and Ireland the Reformation brought not peace, but a sword. The real conquest, which medieval kings never attempted, Henry VIII was compelled to undertake, if his Reformation " empire " was to last. Costly campaigns were soon abandoned for bribery and conciliation, but St. Leger's mild regime of 1540–56 broke down, less on a difference of creeds than of civilizations. The conversion set on foot was not so much of Catholic into Protestant as of elected chiefs into hereditary landlords, of a tribal system to primogeniture and feudal tenures, and of Celtic custom to English common law. It was under the Catholic Mary that its failure was first admitted, and a beginning made with the plantations which were designed to substitute English for Irish proprietors. The everlasting fends of Irish clans, of Geraldines and Butlers, O'Neills and O'Donnells, which had defied the Dublin Government, were changed now for an agrarian revolution, inflamed with racial jealousy and religious propaganda. Shane O'Neill's war of 1563 in Ulster was mixed tribalism and pillage, but the Desmond rising of 1579, which led to the planting of Munster, and the war of 1598–1604 were national and religious rebellions, aided by a Papal blessing and Spanish troops.

The plantation system tried to eradicate Irish civilization through English military colonies; the best blood of Devon was quartered on Munster; Londoners and Scots settled in Ulster. In a military sense, the strong medicine administered by Perrot and Mountjoy succeeded, and here and there an independent genius like the first Boyle, Earl of Cork, or a Scot colony, planted, built, and prospered. But the cost of conquest, physical and moral, was bootless. Spenser, one of the colony whose house was fired by rebels, has told us of the state of Ireland as Elizabeth's soldiers left it; of cannibalism, of wolves, of children eating grass, " anatomies of death," creeping on all fours. Absentee landlords, adventurers who would not work, a Church whose alien service-books did not reach the people—here was a void, filled up by hungry Irish tenantry and Jesuit missions. The Ulster plantation of James' time was oppressive; Government was despoiled, the Church robbed of endowments, and despotism deprived of its sole apology, for Ireland was neither free nor wealthy.

The Elizabethan " commonwealth," which failed thus to solve one problem of empire, was a little England, whose greatness rested on command of the sea. This, for the first time, became the key to English progress, not so much by effort of the Government as from spontaneous, individual, energy. Henry VIII's European policy and Spanish alliance checked any tendency to pursue the paths opened by the Cabots, and it was not till the middle of the century that English commerce launched out on the ocean. The Dudleys and Howards began, earlier, to invest money in Mediterranean trade instead of English land, but the real lead was given by London merchants with Bristol and Western ports close behind. In Elizabeth's reign enormous profits urged and rewarded the Protestant party; large sums were hazarded in sea ventures by Leicester, Walsingham, and all the noble adventurers, the Raleighs, Cumberland, and Gilberts. £5,000 was put up for Drake's circumnavigation of the globe; the profits to the shareholders were £500,000, and to the Queen the same.

At first inspired by gold, then by religion and policy, only last by a conscious colonial scheme, the English tried every opening in new worlds and contested the monopoly of Spain, Portugal, or Venice in the old. Chancellor, seeking a North-East Passage to India, reached Archangel; Jenkinson pushed on to the Volga, the Caspian, and Bokhara; soon the wild Shirleys were living as princes in Persia. Trying a North-West Passage, Davis and Frobisher staked English claims on North America. Hawkins, following others, deported from Guinea and the Gold Coast slaves whom he sold in Spanish America, and taught Drake to defy the preserves assigned by Rome to the Catholic kings. The Spaniards' treacherous attack on his fleet off Vera Cruz in 1568 began that never-ceasing war between Philip and the adventurers, which drifted into a war of nations. The Queen's connivance overcame the opposition of Cecil, his disapproval of piracy, and his reluctance to part with the Spanish alliance. When, after three years spent in forcing entry to the Pacific, sacking the fount of Spain's treasure at Valparaiso, and returning by the Philippines, Java, and the Cape, Drake was knighted in 1581 on the *Golden Hind*, the Crown accepted the New World from its seamen, and the epic age of Elizabeth dawned. We find Englishmen commanding the galleys in Russia, jewellers to Akbar at Delhi, organizing the navy of Japan. Humphrey Gilbert, returning in his ten-ton *Squirrel* from exploring Newfoundland, found heaven near by sea. The heaven, or Valhalla, of fighting men opened in the Azores for Richard Grenville, who there in *Revenge* fought fifty-three Spanish galleons. Piratic war and Calvinism made that heroic temper in England, which pride of race and Catholicism gave to Spanish *conquistadores*. Drake, served in his cabin off silver plate, the violins playing on *Golden Hind*, executing on solitary islands the mutineers with whom he partakes of the Sacrament; Cavendish, sailing up the Thames with sails of blue damask, his crew each with a golden chain, Elizabeth waving

her hand from Greenwich Palace; Hawkins'
slavers, in confident dependence on their
"Almighty God, who never suffereth his
elect to perish"; — every year English
patriotism rose more feverishly as these
extraordinary men, fresh from playing football
with Eskimos or bowls in Panama forests, or
turning neutral traders adrift in mid-ocean,
returned with their gold, ivory, palm oil, and
cinnamon, to sit in the House of Commons
and plan interception of next year's treasure
fleet.

The experience of seamen and merchants
introduced two vital changes in the instruments of English policy : the remodelling of
the Navy and the foundation of commercial
companies. The "great ship" of Henry
VIII, superior to Mediterranean galleys, but
still slow and cumbrous, gave way to flush-
decked smaller ships, which made rings round
the Armada and lasted in type till Nelson's
day. Seamanship and gunnery were taught
by experts, who had bought experience dear in
forty years of ocean warfare. Meanwhile,
charters and statutes set up the joint stock
and regulated companies—Muscovy, Levant,
Eastland, and East India—which massed the
new capital of England for continuous enterprise, and by permanent factories and trading

alliances laid the foundations of empire. The beginnings were precarious, but before the Queen's death Raleigh perpetuated her name in Virginia, fishing fleets were annexing Newfoundland, and Wiltshire factories testing their kerseys on the natives of Bengal.

The new companies' charters, bidding them maintain a high standard of craftsmanship, showed that the Government had inherited an ideal from the guilds. All the characteristic methods of earlier trade policy were continued by Burghley; their characteristic evils had not disappeared, but the methods were more elastically applied and the evils diminished. The Statute of Labourers (1563) aimed at redressing, in a conservative sense, the balance upset by weak government and violent oscillation. Its purpose was to grade the whole working population; to retain the skilled trades for corporate towns, to make apprenticeship the regular avenue to industry, to stabilize employment by standardized conditions of service. Tariffs maintained the staple home industries, while the justices were expected to protect employees by fair wages. Burghley was a mercantilist of more modern type; he looked to bullion less than the balance of trade, less to prohibitive Navigation Acts than to new markets. Government used its power in encouraging new industries and immigration, and the patents or monopolies granted, if sometimes abused by courtiers like Raleigh, on balance did increase the national riches. The suppression of the Hanse privileges and the exhaustion of Venice freed commerce from its oldest rivals. Protestant theology reinforced capitalist theory, in justifying loans at interest as a necessary weapon of extended trade, while bankers and insurance supported the credit that now rested on London, instead of Antwerp.

The land, still the resource of four-fifths of the people, was reaching the equilibrium that lasted for a century. Enclosure went on, but with less violence, and partly for tillage. Policy regarding the food supply was opportunist; the level of prices was watched by royal commissioners, and sales, export, and import, were regulated by the Council in touch with local authorities. The Poor Law of 1601, codifying half a century's experiments, replaced the Church's control of charity by the municipality and parish overseers; distinguishing the vagrant from the unfortunate and " poor in very deed," it made the parish the unit of relief, allowed the principle of a rate in aid, encouraged provision of work for

the workless, and the house of correction for
the vagabond.   Over the whole of this
economic fabric Council and Star Chamber
watched, interfering to protect tenant-right,
insist on fair wages, or stop profiteering.
Their policy was the beginning of the end of
paternal government, but it succeeded in its
main object, to keep the balance of the whole.
Figures of building, statistics of customs
revenue, and the capital sunk in land, prove
the swollen volume of national wealth;
legislation and Council records show its considerable success in achieving an equitable
distribution.   The petty capitalism of the
Domestic system of industry covered the
countryside; the cloths of East Anglia and
Wales were sold at Cairo or Narva with those
of Yorkshire and the Cotswolds; small farmers
and yeomen still marked a deep line in the
subsidy book.

Indictments against whole ages or classes
falsify the workings of nature, but a great
literature declares the gloom in which the
reign departed.   War was raging, severe
plague, heavy taxation, religious discontent.
Nouveaux riches, beggars, sham adventurers,
corruption, and the wisdom of riches, lit up
the sins of a new acquisitive society.   Irish
campaigns made the fortune of victuallers,
gambling on the exchanges with Government

money that of royal servants. The gold was wearing off the apples brought back from the garden of the Hesperides. The bid of young Essex for power failed, but round him there gathered many elements of opposition— Catholics, liberal thinkers, Puritans, lovers of war—and the execution of this spoilt popular figure in 1601 only postponed a day of reckoning.

The nation, however, was still loyal, and its condition vastly better than at the death of Henry VIII. In place of armed magnates, of religious and social chaos, of the knife and forays on the marches, the Queen bequeathed, unsettled but solidifying fast, all that makes up a civilized state. Only partiality or cynicism can dismiss the public spirit of Burghley or Walsingham, the paternal activity of Government, the mass of private benefaction, the assured increase of regard for equal justice, or doubt the existence of a people that centred its commonwealth in the Crown. Against its foes, this Government used torture, spies, censorship, and martial law; to loyal subjects it gave a rule more honest, more even-handed, and more rewarding than any that had gone before. To her last Parliament Elizabeth appealed : " Above all earthly treasure, I esteem my people's love, more than which I desire not to merit."

CHAPTER VI

CHURCH AND STATE

THE House of Commons of 1604 told
James I that he was "misinformed" as to
their privileges; only the Queen's sex and
venerable age, they implied, had stopped
them from asserting their legal authority in
State and Church. During the next thirty
years Puritan common lawyers elaborated
this conservative view of the revolution they
were asking, and successfully convinced posterity that the Stuarts caused civil war by
plotting to subvert an ancient Constitution.
A later generation, who saw in 1640 only a
consecrated halting-place between Magna
Carta and the Reform Bill, darkened this
picture of an executive encroaching on the
legislative power, and it has been left to
modern scholarship, particularly in America,
to demolish the constitutional theory of the
Pilgrim Fathers, and relegate the legend of
" despotic " Stuarts to the same limbo as that
of " parliamentary " Lancastrians.

The constitutional problem of Elizabeth and James should not be viewed through a telescopic lens of 1832, but in the broken light of the medieval Government they inherited. The rule of law in that Government was not the exclusive supremacy of Common Law; indeed the bare idea of a sovereign unity— whether King, Parliament, or one branch of the law—was alien to the fifteenth century. True, in one sense men looked on their Government as unitary, since the executive, legislative, and judicial powers were all centred in the King and Council. But, in another sense, Government was quasi-federal; for the Crown had inherited functions coming from different sources, and was daily acquiring others. Certain powers the King had as Duke of Lancaster, some as head of the feudal structure, others as overlord expected to direct foreign relations and defence, others (under the Tudors) as head of the Church. These functions, in part older than Parliament, but in part arising after the sphere of the Lancastrian Parliament had been more or less determined, were exercised through different agencies of the Crown, such as Admiralty, Chancery, or High Commission. The King's Council might be continuously expanded, by many degrees, from half a dozen experts up to the full meeting of four hundred in the great Council of Parliament, and only custom assigned specific duties to any particular branch of it.

Neither the lawyer nor the ordinary Tudor layman thought of their Government as a despotism, but the checks and balances upon royal authority were negative and medieval. That is to say, Parliament was recognized as the King's Council at its highest pitch, and the Common Law fully protected the elementary rights and properties of all men; a legal champion of the prerogative like Bacon accepted these positions as fully as a fanatic for the Common Law like Coke. But few men, till Coke, would argue that Parliament or Common Law were the sole source of legal authority; the King's prerogatives, in the field not yet covered by Parliament, were viewed as forming part of the law. Cranmer's Litany, after all, omits the infrequent Commons, and asks the congregation to pray only for the Crown, nobility, Council, and magistrates. If Henry VIII was the restoring architect of Parliament, he did not demolish older chambers of government, and distributed the mass of new business involved by the modern state among all his councils and commissioners. Historically, he had undeniable right to delegate powers to branch councils in North and Marches, or to temporary commissions, and no legal objection was taken to Elizabeth's activities as head of the forces or arbiter of foreign policy.

How profoundly this use of an extraparliamentary prerogative affected the man in the street can best be seen in the immense powers given to Justices of the Peace; the Council would tell them to conscript recruits, to force employers to take on discharged soldiers, to fix grain prices, or commandeer carriage. With all such manifold activities of a modern state, statute and common law as yet hardly dealt. But if questions arose of a conflict between prerogative and law, the only court of appeal could be the judges, who attended Parliament as its legal advisers, drafted bills, and approved proclamations. Northumberland thus referred to them Edward VI's last testament, Burghley the Queen's powers under the Supremacy Act and her power to commit prisoners. The Stuarts' constant reference to them was thus warranted and inevitable, for they alone were recognized arbitrators on a fluid constitution, which events were straining beyond endurance.

Renaissance and Reformation, the events in question, were indeed giving to the world new doctrines, which must sooner or later settle

H

this decision of sovereign power. Already
Henry VIII had found it useful to condemn
by statute the recurring fallacy that land
belonged to the people as a whole; already
French thought was teaching that a ruler who
offended the people could be deposed; by
the time of the Petition of Right, the notion
of a contract as the origin of government had
become a commonplace of debate. On the
other side, revived Roman Law armed the
King with Cæsar's inviolate majesty, Machiavelli's " Prince " taught the necessity of
absolutism, the Church's homilies a duty of
passive obedience to the Lord's anointed.
But abstract notions of despotism, while they
inflamed, did not provoke the English contest,
nor did abstract ideals of liberty cause that
rapid advance of Parliament and Common
Law which transformed the constitution in
the late sixteenth century. This change was
due to practical politics and the rule of
Henry VIII.

The Commons' debates in the generations
after 1558, whose startling ability arrests us
in D'Ewes' or Burton's journals, were not the
product of immaturity. A century of classical
education and the open Bible, the same of
strenuous local government, gave political
insight to a class enriched by speculative

commerce and monastic lands. Bereft of
support from Church and nobles, Henry submitted his measures to the bourgeois; the
councillors were brought into Parliament to
carry royal policy, which the Commons thus
learned to discuss with Cromwell or the Cecils.
The Crown's careful selection of Speakers,
candidates, and new constituencies is the
best tribute to the power it had evoked; its
enforced deference to middle-class opinion
soon found an echo in constitutional claims.
The best county families contested elections;
opposition meetings outside Parliament embarrassed Elizabeth; in debate, or through
the Press, they voiced public indignation at
the Government's mercy to the Scottish
Queen, or its rigour to godly ministers. From
the middle of the century fusion between
prerogative and law grew apace. An Act of
Edward VI was held necessary to confirm
Henry's prerogative Court of Augmentations,
and Elizabeth passed her Wardrobe accounts
through the Exchequer. Her ministers were
meticulously respectful to the law, and anticipated in practice the judges' decision of 1610,
that proclamations did not make law, so
much as expound it. The modern lines
between executive and judiciary became clear,
Star Chamber itself almost a law-abiding

public tribunal. With the growth of national unity and secular public opinion, the Common Law courts attacked High Commission, the Court of Requests, and the Northern Council; the Commons questioned the unstatutory basis of the Church, or the royal grants of trading monopolies. A demand for certainty and fixed legal rule was in the air, flooding one by one the compartments of a loose, discretionary, haphazard Constitution. Common Law pressed these innovating claims in the guise of antiquity, a school of legal antiquarians from Coke to Prynne producing from imaginary statutes, or closed Year-books, the precedents which were to justify the ways of revolution.

Their work was to save the country, but it falsified history, and if legality could excuse incompetence, the Stuart cause was impregnable. The main constitutional charges against them were taking ship-money from inland towns, adding impositions (or additional duties) to the tariff, giving monopolies to corporations, punishing soldiers by martial law, dispensing with the law in favour of individuals, and debarring Parliament from touching the Church. But all these powers could be deduced from the Crown's inherited functions, and all were taken as of course by

Elizabeth. She, like the Stuarts, recognized
the Commons' privileges of debate, but none
to " frame a form of religion or a state of
government, as to their idle brains shall seem
meetest." She sent to the Tower private
members who trenched on these mysteries,
and extinguished many private bills. She,
like James, claimed for Chancery the control
of contested elections; her judges, like
Charles', held that the Crown need not show
cause for its arrest of prisoners. If, then,
there was any Tudor constitution, all the
Stuarts did was to try to maintain it, and
though those who thus stand still may cause
a revolution, it is an inexactitude to call
them the revolutionaries.

The wise moderate Puritan, Selden, looking
back during the Civil War, put his finger on
its real cause. " *Scrutamini Scripturas*—
search the Scriptures; these two words have
undone the world." Walsingham's brother-
in-law, Peter Wentworth, did not risk the
Tower for abstract freedom of speech, but for
liberty to attack bishops, whom he viewed
as pseudo-Popes. The Commons refused
supply to James, primarily because he was
too lenient to Catholics and protected High
Commission. Not so much ship-money, as
the barque of Peter, in which room (they felt)

was reserved for Laud, turned passive resistance into active revolt.

Of the forces hostile to Elizabeth's settlement, the Catholics became, after the Armada, almost negligible. Pius V's Bull of 1570 gave them little choice between heresy and allegiance and, coupled with the plots that followed, split them into two camps. There were those—Jesuits, conspirators, and saints —who followed Campion to the scaffold; others, swayed more by secular priests, members of county families, or less devout, either submitted to recusancy fines and more or less easy imprisonment, or by hearing private Masses from some wanderer excused a forced attendance at their parish church. The Gunpowder Plot of 1605 deepened their dissensions. The extremists, infuriated by disappointment at James' illusive promises and inflamed with the spirit which soon plunged Europe into thirty years of war, finally ruined their Church in English eyes. The Commons' rage pressed down guilty and innocent alike in new crushing legislation; eight or nine thousand recusants still witnessed to Catholic religion, but the general loyalty of Catholics to the Crown in the Civil War sharply distinguished them from other enemies of Anglicanism.

The spiritual leaders of Protestantism who survived Mary's persecution did so by flight to Geneva, Frankfort, and other cities of refuge. Thence they returned in 1558, recharged with those views which once before, under Edward VI, had broken up King Henry's settlement. The essence of the reformed Churches they had found abroad was undeviating obedience, as they interpreted it, to the Word of God, which defined not only a pure doctrine, but also the details of Church government, rites, and ceremonies. Between such men and Elizabeth there could be no agreement. She, mainly for political reasons, wished to preserve all she could of the pre-Reformation Church; they, in the name of Christ, now newly revealing Himself, to destroy it root and branch. The preliminary " vestiarian " controversy over the surplice touched, then, only the fringe of a question, which went to the very basis of religion. The Anglican view of Scriptural authority, stated long ago by Thomas Cromwell, distinguished between matters necessary to salvation, for which Scripture provided, and things " indifferent," such as government or ceremonies, which were left to the direction of national Churches. On this theory the controlling voice should be left with the sovereign, to whom the Reformation had restored prerogatives usurped by Rome.

Unity of Church and State was, in some shape, still the universal opinion of Europe, and the common ground of obedience in Elizabeth's early days was that Puritanism meant anarchy. The majority of her first bishops—Jewel, Horne, or Grindal—viewed their office as no divine institution, but as an allowable office of ecclesiastical police; they wore the vestments with reluctance as things distasteful, though " indifferent," and had to be goaded by the Queen into suppressing their more advanced brethren. Her suspension in 1577 of Grindal, Parker's successor at Canterbury, marks the beginning of modern Anglicanism. The spiritual head of the Church was thus dealt with for his failure to suppress " prophesyings," or meetings of clergy and laity to discuss religion, which half the bishops approved. In them Elizabeth saw the germ of Presbyterianism, whose " parity " she sincerely held to be " dangerous to a kingly rule." From the point of view of Tudor government, she was right, though Puritanism in England embraced many more than Presbyterians.

Omitting the " Family of Love " and minor sects that periodically agitated London, Puritans could be divided into three main bodies. Least numerous and important before 1625 were the Independents, earlier called Brownists, after Robert Browne, whose book raised the cry: "A Reformation without tarrying for any." Their principle was each congregation's autonomy; their crime, repudiation of any State supremacy; their merit for the future, a claim for tolerance. It was men of this type who wrote and printed the "Martin Marprelate" libels against the bishops, for which their leaders were brought to execution; Archbishop Whitgift's severity drove the extremists into exile in Holland, whence a remnant in 1620 carried to a New England the ideal Church so unappreciated in the old.

The Presbyterians were more organized, persistent, and formidable. In Geneva, La Rochelle, or Edinburgh they had models and supporters. Their leaders were learned and influential—men like Cartwright, professor of divinity in Cecil's own University of Cambridge, or Travers, the tutor to Cecil's children. Their platform was openly announced in 1572 in the "Admonition to the Parliament"; their tactics were furtive—to stay in the Church, but to recase her decadent system with their own. Presbyterian assemblies met in London. The *classis*, or kirk session, was illegally linked to the Church system in the Midlands and East Anglia. A Dean of Durham, ordained only at Geneva, for twenty years avoided deprivation. In many parishes ministers approved by illegal synods declaimed prayers equally illegal.

Shading into the Presbyterians was the largest section of all, perhaps two-thirds of the laity, who wished a broad Church establishment on Puritan lines. The Queen's ministers were at their head. Cartwright was patronized by Leicester; Walsingham, Knollys and Mildmay instigated, or introduced into Parliament bills against the Prayerbook. No session from 1563 to 1640 passed without some move from the Commons, for relief from ceremonies, and from subscription to the Articles, or for tempering of episcopacy by Presbyterian " assistants; " if the Commons were representative even of the aristocracy, the political majority of England was clearly against Elizabeth's settlement.

The Commons of 1604 disclaimed the name of Puritan, but the ministers for whom they asked relief urged, at the Hampton Court Conference, the association of presbyters with bishops; county petitions demanded reform " agreeable to the example of other reformed churches "—the very formula which in 1643 was to unite Presbyterians of England and Scotland in the Covenant.

Nothing could have long prevented this blending of religious with constitutional opposition, but the anomalies of the Constitution provoked it; and on the question, whether it was a royal or a parliamentary Church, civil war began. It was true that the Six Articles and the Prayer-books were passed through Parliament, but there, in Tudor law and practice, parliamentary co-operation ended. Like her father, the Queen upheld this bare parliamentary scaffolding by royal action. The Supremacy Act empowered her to set up a High Commission, but the Commission's mandate was devised with her bishops. The Act of Uniformity allowed her and Parker to reform ceremonies, but their prerogative Injunctions regulated the dress of the clergy and the position of the altar. An Act of 1571 demanded of the clergy subscription only to such of the Thirty-nine Articles as concerned faith and sacraments; going directly counter to this, she amended them in concert with her prelates, and systematically enforced obedience to them all. Gradually, it became clear that nothing short of attacking the royal supremacy would get for the Commons what they wanted. Nothing less could invalidate, for instance, the canons of 1604 which, assented to by Crown and Convocation, demanded of the clergy a declaration that the Prayer-book contained nothing contrary to God's Word. From about 1590 the common lawyers urged a concerted attack on High Commission. Just as Star Chamber, they argued, was restricted by the statute of 1487, so was this Court tied by the Act of Supremacy, which had given no powers of fine and imprisonment. Repeated declarations of Council and Chancery, basing the Commission's jurisdiction not on statute but on the immemorial supremacy of the Crown, brought the conflict to a head. Whatever the letter of the law, all the fervour of religious men and all the instincts of lawyers were outraged by a half-lay, half-ecclesiastical Court, examining accused clergy upon oath, evicting excellent pastors for non-compliance with prerogative rules, evoking cases from every diocese, searching private houses for suspect books.

It had become, then, a war of first principles, and this in more ways than by conflict of laws. Religious differences in 1560 had turned upon expediency, or mere law and order; by 1600 they revolved round dogma, and exposed deep intellectual contradiction.

The Arminian, or (more familiarly) Laudian, movement began in the field of pure theology with a protest against the Calvinists' rigid pre-destination, and with insistence on the freedom of human will. Revolting from the claim that salvation could be won merely by faith, Laudians returned to the Catholic teaching of the necessity for good works. They contemplated, that is, no church of " saints " justified by a self-known declaration of faith, but one of average human beings, using those works of holiness and those sacraments which were consecrated by sixteen centuries of Christian usage. From individual interpretation of the Book, they returned to the corporate authority of the historic Church; they made reason, and no sudden " jump into glory," the pathway to a saving faith, and held that, in the light of reason, each national Church could regulate those " indifferent " matters, for which Scripture had not clearly provided. Richard Hooker, wisest of English conservative thinkers, began in 1594 the publication of his " Ecclesiastical Polity." He taught that law was the justification of society, that the burden of argument must always lie on the individual who challenges it. The usage of antiquity must occupy the ground until it was demonstrably refuted;

the present generation of Christians bound
together past and future in one spiritual
fellowship. How different the Arminians were
from Elizabeth's first clergy can be seen
from their standpoint on the central question
of Episcopacy, which they made no accidental
or arguable matter of convenience, but *jure
divino*, an Apostolic institution, the essence of
a Church. With Bancroft, who succeeded
Whitgift at Canterbury, and with the saintly
Andrewes, Arminianism began to take the
seats of the mighty. In James' later years
the Calvinist archbishop Abbott was superseded in favour by Laud, and the laity realized,
with indignation, that the national Church was
fast being taken by Crown and clergy, through
means the legality of which could hardly be
contested, further away from Reformation
Protestantism and nearer to Rome.

Within the old fabric of Church and State
two rival theories were thus by 1625 firmly
established, and imperative reasons demanded
decision. The balance of constitutional
powers, so long preserved by economic pro-
vincialism, by fixed ideas of custom, by
loyalty born of imminent national peril, was
upset by the weight of modern government.
The unity, publicity, and legalism, which the
Tudors accomplished, broke down the de-

partmental system they had inherited. Yorkshire was now raised to the level of London, the Church was aligned with Parliament, and the public opinion, hitherto confined to one part of political life, was claiming to control all. The greatest constitutional question a country can face was coming to a head; whether one law shall be supreme over all causes and all persons, and, if so, who shall make it.

Which of the rival systems—prerogative and an Anglo-Catholic church, or Parliament, Common Law, and Calvinism—gave fairer promise for freedom and progress, was another question; less susceptible perhaps of a simple answer. But in any case the Tudor Commonwealth, that had walked so delicately on unasked and unanswered questions of principle, must disappear, now that these questions were raised; King and Church were opposed to individual religion and Common Law.

CHAPTER VII

THE FIRST TWO STUARTS, 1603–42

Long continuance of Government's outward forms often masks internal revolution, and the identity of the Stuarts' aims with those of Elizabeth was not inconsistent with sharp differences in method, efficiency, and atmosphere.

It is true that their difficulties were inherited from the Queen, and that Parliament from the first took the aggressive. The finances demanded retrenchment and reform. Between 1588 and 1603 taxation had been thrice as great as in the whole preceding thirty years; the Irish wars bequeathed a heavy debt; standing revenues were depreciated by change in values and diminished by sale of Crown lands. The Commons, insistent on religious reform, refused to fill the gap, and to them was due the lasting poverty of the Stuarts, which in its turn had for a century such far-reaching political effects. Claiming from 1603 to control religion, the Commons also extended their " privileges " to lengths never allowed by Elizabeth—to foreign policy and initiation of public bills.

Nor can history agree that the cause of freedom and justice was wholly bound up with the victory of a narrow, bitter, and class-conscious Parliament. They rejected with petulance proposals for Anglo-Scottish Union. Their treatment of Catholics was brutal, and a jingo Protestantism represented their foreign policy. Of those whom posterity must judge the great minds of the age, a majority—Bacon, Hooker, Strafford, Shakespeare, Hobbes—were enlisted on the side of authority, which was attacked for what justly may be viewed as its good points, as well as for its bad. Administratively, the Government had much to commend it. The Council was active in keeping the balance of classes, in maintaining wages and employment, in reducing prices. The radical Levellers' grievances after 1649 show how little the Puritan political class cared for democracy; the lot of Catholics and Episcopalians, the hollowness of their toleration; "the curse of Cromwell," the solution offered to Ireland; the extinction of the drama, their lop-sided civilization; the free rein given to individualist capitalism, the negative contribution of Puritan religion to social welfare.

I

But in days of Parliamentary and individual growth paternal authority can only be preserved by constant strength, skill, and sympathy. These were now lacking, and nothing is more startling than the solid national opposition found in 1640. The Stuarts were aliens; so were their favourites, Somerset or the Hamiltons. James' costly and squalid Court dispelled the glamour and mystery that enshrined Elizabeth; his unbusinesslike habits made ridiculous the claims which a pedantic scholarship put forward for the divine right of Kings. The Queen, partly owing to her sex, ruled Parliament from the inside through ministers of proved parliamentary power; the Stuarts hectored it from without by new-made peers or favourites, leaving a series of pedestrian secretaries to debate with Eliot, Pym, and the acutest of common lawyers. In an age which reverenced birth, the oldest and most powerful families were affronted. Whereas Elizabeth had created eight peerages, James made sixty, selling many as he sold baronetcies, for cash down. Landed interests were disturbed by revival of obsolete taxes and drastic fines for encroachment on half-forgotten forests. Like Henry VIII, Charles prevented Opposition peers from attending Parliament. When the

war came, the peers who resisted the Crown
or stood neutral included the bulk of the
names—Percy, Russell, Sidney, Cecil, Rich,
Herbert, Devereux, Montague, Cavendish—
which had won most glory under the Tudors.

Economic grievances quickened in the
trading classes the hostility bred by Puritanism. The struggle from 1604–14 over impositions and tariffs left the shadow of legal
victory to the Crown, and unquestionably
the judges, in maintaining its right, whether
directly or through a chartered company, to
levy duties on any commodity, could quote
Tudor example. But the common lawyers
in Parliament contested their law, while
practical reasons made their decision intoler-
able. For the Customs were the one expanding
source of revenue, and four-fifths of them were
raised at London, the spiritual centre of
opposition. Moreover, the industrial fabric
was becoming too complex for conciliar control, and James' well-meant effort to direct the
vital cloth trade by proclamation may well
be one root of the solid Parliamentarianism
of clothing districts in the war. Nor was
this paternal authority even incorrupt; the
monopolies granted in soap, saltpetre, wines,
or alehouses, led directly to peculation and
oppression. Interlopers began to challenge

the chartered companies' monopoly in the
East Indies, Baltic, and Levant. Enter-
prising capitalism broke at a hundred points
from the Government's control. Merchants
used against it the new weapon of financial
credit, which they had freely loaned to
Elizabeth, and drove the King back on further
use of a strained prerogative.

For if on the letter of the law the Stuarts'
case, till 1629 at least, must be held impregnable, it belied the spirit of the Constitution.
Governments are not commonly ruined by
strong action, but by weak action joined to
strong words, and the bark of the Stuarts and
their advisers roused at least as much sense of
injury as their bite. It was one thing for
Elizabeth to deny freedom of debate in some
particulars; a very different to reiterate,
like James, that all privilege was a matter of
revocable royal grace. Expensive currants
seemed more indigestible when judges had
pronounced the power of levying impositions
to proceed from an absolute authority above
law. Men who from 1634 onwards, when coal
ships and Channel packets were intercepted by
corsairs, recognized the need of financing the
navy, felt differently when the King was
declared sole judge of national danger and of
the means to avert it. The Tudors did not

compare questioning of their prerogative to atheism; they had not avowed that they owed account to God alone, nor that ministers were answerable only to themselves. They did not, like Laud, ostentatiously promote divines who preached absolutism, even extending to taxation. No bull, not even John Bull, can bear an indefinite trailing of the red flag; it was this everlasting rehearsal of " a logic which left no man anything he might call his own," which infuriated a generation devoted to individual property and individual religion.

Till 1629 the Crown, asserting legal precedents, kept up a long course of rearguard actions. It maintained its Church powers by the help of High Commission, and its right of levying impositions by that of the ordinary judges. This undecided struggle between prerogative and common law was impersonated in the memorable rivalry between Francis Bacon and Edward Coke, which reached its climax in the elevation of the first to be Chancellor and the dismissal of the second from the Bench. Springing from the same bed of Tudor official compromise, they were rapidly separated by James' quarrel with parliament; Bacon, once a House of Commons man, to pin upon prerogative all his ambitions

of legal, religious, and Imperial reform,—
Coke, once Elizabeth's Attorney, to restrict
legality to common law and statute. In their
contest Bacon made law subservient to arbitrary politics, Coke twisted history to con-
struct an arbitrary rule of law; each, clap-
ping the telescope to his blind eye, saw clearly
half the truth. In the end Parliament, taking
Bacon's teaching of sovereignty and Coke's
legal basis, made a fusion of their views, but
this was still far distant. For the present,
as in the impeachment of Bacon and the
monopolists in 1621, or in the controversy
over the Commons' refusal of revenues for
Charles' life, each side made a negative and
unsatisfying appeal to "the law," to that
body of ancient customs and "fundamentals"
descending from times unconcerned with
unitary and legal sovereignty. Of this the
Petition of Right (1628) was clear proof.
The grievances were glaring and generally
admitted; unparliamentary taxation, billet-
ing of soldiers, martial law, and imprisonment without showing cause. But save the
first, these were the very powers which any
State must possess in emergency. Merely to
deprive the King of them, or disavow (like
Pym) the existence of sovereignty, was the
constitutionalism of the ostrich: especially
when the judges did not accept the Petition

as a statute at all. If such powers were so inherent in sovereignty that "no acts of Parliament make any difference," the real point at issue was, in whose hands they should be. The year 1629, which saw the stormy dissolution of Charles' third Parliament, is vital in history, for upon this point of sovereignty a section, stronger as yet in talent than number, left the opposition for the Crown, and prepared the birth of parties.

"The grand apostate" of this group was Wentworth, later Earl of Strafford, who represents the first phase of royalism on its good and its bad side. He was apostate only in the sense that he would advance no further; for his early career was passed in attacking Buckingham, the "Haman" who stood for wasteful foreign adventures and crude illegality. Wentworth wished to vindicate England's "ancient and sober liberties," but in declaring the law in 1628 he insisted there must be left a discretionary power with the executive. Parliament was "the old and beaten way," but *salus populi, suprema lex;* the King was *pater patriae,* and individual liberty must yield to common good. Hating war and loving strong government, he saw in the Crown the keystone of the arch. His later experience as President of the Northern Council and Deputy in Ireland deepened the conviction that government was " going downhill," pushed down by riotous gentry, or the Irish landlords, whom he compared to Turkish pashas. He disdained to see the common lawyers " snuffle upon " the flowers of the prerogative, which were to be used, as they were by himself in Council and in Ireland, for defence of the lowly and destruction of great offenders. In the " Pyms, Bens, and Prynnes " of Puritanism he could see nothing but anarchy or spiritual arrogance. Some day, power would come full into play; meantime, the King must cherish the prerogatives inseparable from the idea of the State; his servants must hew, and fend, and toil for justice and order; " less than Thorough will not do it."

The " cancerous malignity," which Strafford would cut out of the State, went far deeper in the Church, and the task of Laud was more hopeless. His ideal was that of Henry VIII—the English Jerusalem " as a city at unity with itself; " his intellectual background that of the older Arminians, of a Church grounded in reason, law, and antiquity. He believed that an outward uniformity would bring about spiritual union, and that decency in public worship would redouble the compelling attraction of Catholic truth. His

moral courage was great; he was not afraid
to pillory sin in high places, or to protest
against enclosures by the Crown. Unhappily,
his religion was not tempered with common
humanity, nor his fine ends by any discrimina-
tion in means. To make Bishop Juxon
Treasurer and many clerics justices seemed
to him an important triumph. His sentence
in Star Chamber was always for punitive fines
and mutilation; the God he adored allowed
him to divide husbands from wives and
children, or chase down even in the Colonies
the emigrants his severity had made. With
dubious legality, he enforced the railing in of
altars and bowing at the Sacred Name, and
forcibly put down lectureships, which Puritan
funds had endowed to eke out the spiritual
poverty of parish churches. He ruined
Hooker's appeal to reason by the methods of a
Provost martial, and rested the Church's cause
on a State jurisdiction which every day was
more challenged. The Puritan charge of
Romanising was entirely false of his personal
leanings, but nothing could be more natural;
for reunion with Rome was in the high
Anglican air; it was discussed with Papal
legates in London; conversions to Rome
were fashionable and constant.

So long as opinion in England is free, men

will always think differently of Laud and
Strafford. Their aims were lofty, their personal influence on their age profound, and
much of their teaching against bad aspects
of individualism has had lasting effect. But
on the whole it is fair, perhaps, having seventeenth-century England in mind, to say of
both what Clarendon said of Laud, " a man
unfit for the state of England." For England
was not Ireland, and Milton's generation could
not be retained by the material swaddling
bands which had done duty under Henry
VIII; whatever unity could be achieved must
come through the spirit, and rest on an
informed free opinion.

The doom of Thorough came all the more
surely because England was become politically
one with Scotland and Ireland, and intel-
lectually with Europe; it was their foreign
policy which lost the Stuarts their prestige,
that last raiment to cover the nakedness of a
despotic land. The peace of 1604 with Spain
was a financial necessity, and honourable in its
terms, and till the death of Salisbury and
Prince Henry in 1612 there was weakness,
but no irremediable blunder. Thereafter
foreign policy, as conducted by James,
Charles, and their favourite George Villiers,
Duke of Buckingham, was irresolute, reckless,

and unsuccessful. James' motives were
worthy, for he would be the peace-maker of
Europe, but impracticable, since he hoped to
bury religious division. The Thirty Years'
War broke out in 1618; it was brewing since
the murder of Henry of Navarre in 1610,
which delivered France to a weak regency, and
Europe to the Hapsburgs' Catholic crusade.
With incurable optimism James planted a foot
in either camp. His daughter Elizabeth, the
darling of the country, married Frederick,
Elector Palatine, head of German Calvinists,
who accepted the Bohemian crown from
Austrian rebels: for his son Charles, James
planned marriage with a Spanish Infanta.
English embassies, unsupported by ships or
men, advertised to Europe the weak philan-
thropy of the English King, whose vacillations
and suspicion of his Parliament were inflamed
by Gondomar, the sinister Spanish ambassador at London. Spanish and anti-Spanish
factions disordered the Council; whatever
the previous factiousness of Walter Raleigh,
whose thirst for power had led him in 1603–4
into sedition, his execution in 1618, after a
last fatal voyage to Guiana, was interpreted as
a sacrifice to the will of Spain, whose spoils he
had laid at the feet of Elizabeth. Bankrupt
of resources, James hoped to recover the

Palatinate, of which Spanish troops robbed his daughter, by a Spanish marriage for his son, and the wild ride of Charles and Buckingham to Madrid showed the criminal levity of English rulers. For the match turned upon rights of worship for Catholics which no Parliament would concede; it was broken off on the Palatinate question and Buckingham's personal quarrels with the Spaniards; it was followed by a popular, but senseless war.

The first years of Charles saw the process repeated with France. We get the marriage with Henrietta Maria, with concessions for Catholics which could neither be enforced nor forgotten; help sent to France against the Huguenots; grandiose subsidies and alliances with Denmark and Protestant Germany; war with France over the right of search in the Channel, over English contact with Protestant La Rochelle, and Catholic disappointment arising from the marriage; futile expeditions to Cadiz and Flanders. In the end Buckingham, the tragic comedian of English statesmanship, was murdered by a fanatic who had missed promotion, and in 1629 a dishonourable peace was patched up with both France and Spain. For the next twenty years England ceased to count in Europe. Richelieu treated with contempt Charles' plans for restoration of his nephew in the Palatinate; Spaniards and Dutch fought out their quarrel in English territorial waters; the Dutch alliance was lost in commercial rivalry. Despatches were loaded with possible alliances, but a King of England who had quarrelled with his Parliament was not worth even a scrap of paper. But Europe counted in Protestant England. In his fens Cromwell heard how the Swedish hero Gustavus had fallen, how Protestantism was threatened in Holland, and almost extinguished in Germany. To the Puritans the spirit incarnate of this evil was the gay beauty, Henrietta Maria, who in peace, as later in war, damaged her devoted husband's credit with his people. The Mass in her chapel scandalized London, which feared a repetition in England of the Jesuits' triumph abroad.

Scotland and Ireland were nearer dangers; in them the Opposition's fevered imagination descried armies of kernes and Highlanders being prepared to overthrow the Reformation. But the Crown's position in Ireland was, in hard fact, desperate. When Strafford went there in 1633 he discovered, as Henry Sidney had in Elizabeth's time, two races warring in the bosom of one country, and each a threat to royal supremacy. For much of its weakness, and most of the misery of the Catholic Irish, came from the new Protestant ascendancy, who had flocked in with the plantations. O'Mores and O'Connors could still raise a riot of evicted Irishry, but the Boyles, Annesleys, and other great " undertakers " had hold of the land (much belonging properly to the Church), the offices, and the legislature. Their ascendancy, however congenial to Protestant England, meant injustice to Ireland, hence bloodshed, hence an army, and thence excessive expenditure. Partly, then, in English interests, but with real indignation at the rapacity of these " ravens," Strafford began the herculean toil of making Ireland a royal province, evenly balanced between Protestant and Catholic, self-sufficient and self-defending. Often stultified by Charles' grants and favouritism, he drove by reckless short cuts towards his end. He wanted Ireland securely knit to England ; therefore, with too much breach of faith, he proposed to " plant " Galway. He wished her prosperity ; by tariffs, monopolies, and subventions, he quadrupled her revenues. He wanted her Anglican ; therefore he suppressed the Scottish Presbyterians of Ulster. The events of 1641 showed on what a razor edge of hatreds he had walked. A stream of

protests from Protestant landowners contributed to his impeachment. The "as-
cendency," left to themselves, drove the
Irish to begin the agrarian war of 1641, which
ended in racial massacre. Puritan England
concluded that the Arminian faction round
the King had instigated a tragedy which was,
if successful, next to be played in England;
grimly they tightened their belts to deal, as
Cromwell wrote halfway through the process,
with "these barbarous wretches, who have
imbrued their hands in so much innocent
blood." The King's truce with the Irish in
1643 finally condemned him; Irishwomen
were killed in cold blood at Naseby by the
Puritan troops.

But the immediate occasion of the Stuarts'
ruin came from their native land. James
had reached England in 1603, fresh from a
first victory over Scottish Presbytery, "which
agreeth as well with monarchy as God with
the devil." The cause of God, thus measured
in terms of Episcopacy, made fair progress
for the rest of his reign. The Articles of
Perth (1618) tried to enforce kneeling at
Communion; a High Commission was set up
for Scotland, while the consecration of the
Scottish "constant moderators" by English
bishops revived the Apostolic Succession,

which the Presbyterian fathers, Knox and Melville, hoped they had destroyed. Economic prosperity, which accompanied this despotism, would only ensure peace so long as the nobles and lairds continued their support to the Crown or their neutrality, but all hope of this disappeared when Charles, in his first year, passed the Act of Revocation, withdrawing from them such grants of Church land as they had received since 1542. Their passion for the pure Gospel, thereby revived, was stimulated in 1636–7 by the spread of Laudianism over the Border; Canons and Prayer-book on the English model were issued for Scotland, without approval from the Scottish Church or Scottish Parliament. The nation revolted, seized the royal castles, and in the Solemn League and Covenant (1638) swore, " in the great name of the Lord our God," to finish with bishops. But to abolish them, as demanded by the Church Assembly, would upset the composition of the Lords of the Articles, the committee of Estates on which the Crown had heretofore relied for its veto, and the first Pacification, signed at Berwick in 1639, broke down upon the constitutional and military guarantees which Scotland demanded to safeguard her religion.

At this, its first serious test, the system of Thorough collapsed; the national machine

refused to function further, without a heart.
The money asked from the City, in absence of
Parliament, was refused, and could only be got
from Catholics and clergy; the militia's
ardour to tear down altars showed that
sacerdotalism, not Scotland, was the popular
enemy; Strafford's recall from Ireland, to
take command at home, soon proved that he
alone had kept Ireland tranquil. The Short
Parliament, called on his advice in March
1640, refused supply till ship-money and
arbitrary government were abandoned, and
was quickly dissolved at the signs of its
Scottish sympathies. Undeterred by this
revelation of the public opinion, which for
eleven years he had silenced, Charles pressed
on with his " Bishops' war "; only the rout
of his army on the Tyne and the Scots'
occupation of Newcastle and Durham drove
him to take the advice given by a Council of
Peers to recall Parliament. In November the
Long Parliament assembled, not for twenty
years to be wholly dispersed.

Revolution, with a pall of feverish fears,
hung over England for the next eighteen
months; the Queen's appeals to Rome, army
plots, Irish rebellion, dread of Catholic invasion, fact and magnified fiction, exciting
Parliament and City, gave a handle to the
skilful leadership of Pym and Hampden.

K

But, when due allowance is made for this panic, the unanimity for six decisive months of this purely aristocratic Parliament is the real indictment of Charles, Strafford, and Laud. Falkland, who was to die for Charles at Newbury; or Capel, who died on the scaffold; Hyde, soon to be his minister—these and many such joined hands with Pym's associates, to pass the Acts against Star Chamber and High Commisssion, to secure triennial Parliaments and abolish ship-money, to suppress Laudianism and to impeach Strafford. Financially, the Scots' encampment in England put Charles at Parliament's mercy, which thereby was able to force his assent to an Act making it indissoluble, save by its own consent. Neither this, nor the attainder of Strafford and his execution in May 1641, served to create a Royalist party; that was due to a growing conviction that the extremists meant not to reform episcopacy, but destroy it; not to assert the law, but to claim popular sovereignty.

Collision between the majority of the Lords and the majority of the Commons, made inevitable by religious difference, was precipitated by events outside Parliament. The King's visit to Scotland partly succeeded in its design of winning support which could be used to intimidate England. In October news came of the wholesale massacre of the English in Ireland, a prologue, or epilogue, in Puritan eyes, to the English army plots. The extreme Opposition had not won half of what they asked in religion, for which their remedy was " root and branch;" the moderates did not trust Charles to stand by the concessions he had made. Ireland's troubles alone raised the question of the army command; could it be left safely with Charles, who was ready, so it appeared, to throw an army upon Westminister? In the Grand Remonstrance, therefore, passed and published by the Commons in November, they not only appealed from King and Lords to the nation, but claimed the parliamentary appointment of ministers, and the settlement of religion by a national synod. Charles' culpable attempt in January 1642 to arrest five of the ringleaders drove the Commons to further extremes; by the Militia ordinance of March they asked control of the forces, by the Nineteen Propositions of June, the whole machine of government.

The old Law, so long stinted by Charles' prerogative, he had in 1641 allowed to be reaffirmed; now he could claim to be defending the legal order in Church and State against a faction in religion and the sovereignty of the Commons.

CHAPTER VIII

THE CIVIL WARS, 1642–9

THE character of Charles I, which so largely
provoked war, did much to prolong it, and to
ruin a cause which had in it many elements of
strength. A King on the defensive during
revolution may legitimately use weapons not
commendable in times of peace, and it is idle
to censure Charles for trying to play Presbyterians and Parliament against the Independent army. His fault, rather, was that incurable perversity of judgment, which made him
prefer Henrietta's advice to Clarendon's, which
led to moves behind the backs of his ministers,
like Glamorgan's mission to the Catholic Irish,
or hopeless combinations of English Cavaliers
and Scottish presbyters. Nor could he judge
a man; he conceived that Cromwell could be
won by an earldom, and subordinated his best
advisers, like Hertford or Hopton, to the
peevish Rupert or the brutal Grenville. Yet,
there was about him a fixity of principle which,
when a prisoner and unaided, he wielded like

a weapon of steel. To break prison, he would
make promises he would not keep, or juggle
with soldiers who could break him like an egg-
shell, but he would never extinguish by concession all hopes of recovering the Crown and
the Church as received from his father. Here
at least he defied the promptings of his wife,
who urged him to win Scotland and half England by accepting Presbyterianism; between
two heresies, this Catholic Queen preferred one
commanding an immediate power of the sword.
The King's decision which, with Laud's death
on the scaffold, saved Anglicanism, was thus
of vast import to later history, and his royal
conviction, that revolution could never per-
manently prosper, hedged about with new
divinity the idea of kingship and projected it
forward for another thirty years.

Civil War England was not, as Henry VII's,
a group of separate provinces and, thanks to a
century of strong government and the printing
press, no geographical line divided the parties.
The ultra-royalist Duchy of Cornwall contained
many Puritans; Puritan London and Essex
produced Cavalier soldiers and conspirators.
It is, broadly speaking, true that the trading
classes were Puritan; since ports and industrial markets were more numerous south and
east of a line taken from Hull to Southampton,

this area was predominantly Puritan, while North and West were the reverse. But economic and class divisions were no more rigid than geography, and it was never a struggle of rich against poor. Half the peerage did not support Charles, and at least half of the squires were Puritan. The war was feudal rather than social, if feudalism means the leadership of a recognized aristocracy. Parliament began by vowing to " live and die with the Earl of Essex," and Puritan Saye and Sele could raise Oxfordshire against the University, a Puritan Herbert led Wiltshire, a Cavalier Somerset the Welsh March.

But essentially men were fighting, less for men, class, or shire than for firmly-held views of law and religion. Diverse ideals had always been implicit in Renaissance and Reformation, and had branched further apart by force of events, or unnatural repression. The classical revival, which produced the despotic teaching of Italy and Roman law, had also discovered in Plutarch and Athens an idealized aristocratic republicanism; not only individual liberty, but the State's divine right, had come out of the Reformation. Educated Englishmen, long apprenticed by debate and printed controversy to these high notions, were divided into two parties by far more than material

interests. The wide ramifications of the
Court, poetry and drama, the classic tradition,
chivalry, mysticism, reverence for degree and
order, all those catholic feelings which make
men feel themselves part of an ancient country,
a universal creed, or a great society,—such
sentiments produced the Cavalier. On the
other side were the lovers of personal liberty,
whether it were based on law or abstractions—
the traders, fanatics, common lawyers, classic
republicans, and all those Protestant indivi-
dualists who resented governmental centraliza-
tion, hierarchy of rank, and cramping of the
spirit by human ordinance. To antiquity the
Puritans opposed energy, to honour truth, to
sentiment reason, to the glory of warrior and
song the aspirations of every humble seeker and
finder.

But rigid lines between English parties are
drawn less by statesmen than by historians,
and in this most merciful of civil wars there
were none. Many men of intellect or position
entirely abstained; all went into it unwillingly,
and the New Model army was half composed
of conscripts. There were, of course, pure
politicians like Shaftesbury or Holland, who
crossed and recrossed from one side to the
other, but there were also legal Puritans of the
Selden type who hated sects, and Cavaliers

like Sunderland who disliked bishops.   There
were Anglican parsons who kept their parishes
under a Presbyterian system, and ex-Cavaliers
who joined the New Model.   Finally, the wars
were closed by Monk, who had served loyally
in each camp.   The margin, then, between
the rivals was narrow and fluctuating; many
families were divided, even the Cromwells;
and in this " war without an enemy " (as the
Puritan general Waller wrote to the Royalist
Hopton) peace was never far away.

The grounds for the Puritans' overwhelming military victory could be predicted from a
study of Elizabethan England.   Their secure
possession of London and the rich southern
shires was half the battle.   Two-thirds of
English trade circulated from London, and
there two-thirds of the customs were collected.
The very spectacle of Parliament and law
courts, sitting as of old at Westminster, seemed
to put the onus of aggression on the King.
The Inns of Courts were the real university of
the lawyers who rejected prerogative; the City
was the mother of an active Press, of a wealthy
Presbyterianism, and of trained bands who
formed the only exception to the undisciplined
amateur soldiership of the day.   With London
and commerce went the fleet, which under its
commanders, Northumberland and Warwick,

incorporated much of the Elizabethan Protestant spirit. By land Parliament held the
inner military lines, by sea they commanded
the circumference, and steadily crushed Royalist hopes of European assistance, and Royalist
bases in Ireland and the Channel isles. Trade
and the City enabled Parliament to pay and
equip a regular army, while the Cavaliers
scrambled for contributions from great magnates, Oxford college plate, or sale of Crown
jewels.

But the greatest military asset of Parliament
was Puritanism itself. Were they not the
elect—" a people with a stamp set upon them
by God," said Cromwell—" His people, who
are the apple of His eye, for whom even Kings
shall be reproved? " They had much to
avenge. Eliot, dead in the Tower, and refused even burial in Cornwall,—" whose blood
still cries for vengeance "; Prynne and Bast-
wick with their ears gone, exiles in America,
godly preachers deprived, massacre in Ireland.
But now the sword was in their hand. " O
how comely it is," wrote Milton years later,

> " and how reviving
> To the spirits of just men long oppressed,
> When God into the hands of their deliverer
> Puts invincible might
> To quell the mighty of the earth, the oppressor."

Now they could win that perfect reformation of which Elizabeth had robbed their fathers; the wild beast Strafford was trapped and slain, and Canterbury in the Tower. Religious democracy, long held under, foamed over in what Bossuet called " mille sectes bizarres,"— Independents, Fifth Monarchy men, and Quakers, Anabaptists, Socinians, or Ranters. Idealists and adventurers from New England, Henry Vane and Downing, returned to make their game in the revolution. A countless pamphlet literature vented the rights of men in a state of nature, human equality, and popular sovereignty. The Puritans' mental energy impressed their bitterest foes for more than a generation. Confident of their calling, they came from the plough or workshop to command armies and fleets; agriculture, economics, building, law, all felt the afflatus; Restoration England had still to submit to their intellectual lead. Of such material Oliver Cromwell, a Huntingdon squire, typical of hundreds in that age of noble blood but limited income, formed the army of the Eastern Associated counties; officered by gentlemen, picked without respect for religious orthodoxy, but Godfearing men of the sort Oliver preferred, " a plain russet-coated captain, who knows what he fights for, and loves what he knows."

But in the first three years of war such troops were rare, and the outcome consequently doubtful. Edgehill, the first serious battle (October 1642) was indecisive; disappointed in his first dash for London, Charles fell back on Oxford; for another year and more these two capitals, each the rallying-place of a Parliament, a civilization, and armies, disputed England with alternating success. The royal forces were dissipated in the country-house warfare congenial to too many of their magnates; the King's strategy of a triple advance upon London broke down on the refusal of the Cornish army to carry their triumph beyond Wiltshire, and in the failures to take Hull and Gloucester. Before Pym died he won the Scottish army to support Parliament; a high proportion of its officers had been trained in Continental war, while its leader, Leven, was a considerable general. The political price paid was high, for the league of September 1643 pledged England to Presbyterianism, but its military justification was seen in the greatest battle of the war, Marston Moor (July 1644), which delivered the North to Parliament. On the other hand, Essex was beaten in the West, Montrose was raising the Highlands in the Scots' rear, and a third year closed without a verdict.

Petty garrisons on opposite hills, provincial

levies, even of grouped counties, and skirmishes like that at Chalgrove, where Hampden was mortally wounded, could not decide the war. For this a regular army was needed, mobile, paid, and under unified command, and only Parliament had the means and fervour to make it. Pressed by Cromwell, the Committee of both Kingdoms, the liaison body for England and Scotland, recommended to Parliament the formation of a " New Model " army of 22,000 men; the commander was Fairfax, with powers of naming his officers, and Cromwell its lieutenant-general. At Naseby (June 1645) they destroyed the last considerable royal army. For a year longer Charles lived the life of a hunted partridge between Oxford, the Cotswolds, and Wales, but steadily the lines round him grew nearer, and in May 1646 he surrendered himself to the Scots, who already at Philiphaugh had disposed of Montrose. Oxford fell the next month; only the Scilly Isles, Jersey, and one or two Welsh castles still flew the royal flag.

Three summers more were to pass before the King's head was held up at Whitehall, to the rolling of drums that drowned the groans hailing the Commonwealth of England. The Revolution, like all revolutions, had fallen to pieces. More than discontent with inefficiency had caused the replacement of Essex and Manchester by Fairfax and Cromwell. They were " grandees," suspect of wishing to avoid the arbitrament of war, or the fall of monarchy. Most of all, the Puritans were divided by religion. A great majority in Parliament never intended to relax the " golden reins of discipline "; their Church, as they had argued under Elizabeth, was the true Church of England, purged of prelacy. Presbyterianism proper was not the ideal of the early leaders, Pym or Hampden, but military necessity brought them to it. The Westminster Assembly, set up in 1643, and soon reinforced by Scottish ministers, proposed the full presbyterian model, but the English common lawyers insisted on giving final powers to an Erastian body of parliamentary commissioners, and the Independents contested every inch. For, while Independency could only breathe in an air of toleration, the Presbyterians and their Scottish friends demanded the suppression of heresies. Internecine war raged in the assembly, on the liberty of separate congregations, the powers of lay elders, exclusion from the Sacrament, and preaching of laymen, while each body of theologians looked for support to an army in the field.

The lull of peace gave Charles the chance of recovering what he had lost in war. The terms so far offered by the Presbyterian majority in Parliament, in the propositions of Uxbridge (1644) and Newcastle (1646), were impossible; he was asked to surrender the Church and militia, to transfer control of the executive, and to proscribe long lists of his best friends. But in February 1647 the Scots gave him up to the English, and a contest opened between Presbyterians and Independents for the control of his person; short of his death or deposition, for which few were yet prepared, the Crown's weight must tilt the scales. The ideals of Parliament were better than their methods. As a preliminary to peace, they were resolved to rid themselves of the dictatorship of soldiers, to disband the bulk of the New Model, and to form a new force for service in Ireland. But the pay they offered to the old army was miserably inadequate, and they proposed to officer the new by Presbyterians alone. Threatened with loss of temporal prospects and spiritual freedom, the army mutinied, and under the agitators, the elected delegates from each regiment, broke from the restraining influence of Cromwell and his son-in-law Ireton, who now had the alternative of abandoning their men, or of

guiding an army which was resisting the civil
power.

Reluctantly, and impelled by their followers,
the army commanders in June 1647 seized
the King at Holmby and the artillery at
Oxford, marched on London, purged Parliament of its most obnoxious Presbyterians, and
in the "Heads of the Proposals" produced
their plan for a settlement. Mainly the work
of Ireton, the Heads resemble most nearly the
solution gradually devised in the two next
centuries; in effect, they would have subjected
not only the King but a biennial parliament to
new and representative constituencies, and
have checked an uncoercive episcopal Church
by general toleration for Protestants.

But this philosophic radicalism commanded
adherence neither from King, Parliament, nor
civilian Independents. Confronted by this
all-powerful army, the first two naturally drew
together, and for a year the King bargained to
win those elements of moderate civilian support which would give best military and constitutional guarantees. Escaping from one
captivity at Hampton Court to another at
Carisbrooke, in December he signed the
"Engagement" with the Scottish nobility.
In return for Presbyterianism in Scotland and
(for three years at least) in England, with

special concessions as to place and office for Scotsmen, the terms restored to Charles his command of the army, his choice of councillors, and royal veto; no toleration was to be given to Independents, or any sects. Once more Scottish theology imperilled the civil liberties of England, and from the Engagement sprang the second Civil War (May to September 1648).

In the military sense it was a promenade. Fairfax crushed the Royalists in Kent and Essex; Cromwell dealt with Presbyterian colonels in Wales and, with Lambert, broke Hamilton's straggling army of " Engagers " at Preston. Both staunch Presbyterians and loyal Cavaliers disliked this insincere alliance; the Independents, judging Presbyterians who joined it as men who sinned against the light, viewed the second war as infinitely baser than the first, being designed to " vassalize us to a foreign nation." In the army's absence, Parliament again approached the King, but with different programmes voiced by different sections. Holles implored him to concede Presbyterianism; even Vane, the Independents' ablest civil brain, to Cromwell's horror was " meddling with the accursed thing." A dour suspicion possessed the army, that they had been tricked into sin by negotiation with

Charles. Their council, before they set out to war, rang with denunciation : " We have gone about," said one orator, " to wash a blackamoor." Waves of fundamentals and natural rights broke on the devoted head of Ireton, who defended common law and private property. Before dispersing, the soldiers agreed to call to account, on their return, " that man of blood " Charles Stuart.

The mind of their leader moved slowly; he had taken little part in public life till he was over forty, and had lived much alone. He had stuck to Parliament while it offered a chance of settlement; he had deprecated the march on London, and warned extremists " that which you get by force is nothing." He was not, he admitted, " wedded or glued " to any form of government, though now, as always, he preferred something with monarchy in it. He would rather wait for the decision of " some extraordinary dispensation." As the campaign moved on, Providence bulked larger than ever in his heart. " Look at providences, they hang so together; " this army, the poor godly people raised by God, invincible. He would not rest on arguments of *salus populi*, but Providence beckoned the army on, forward to a real settlement of righteousness, not to any " ruining, hypocritical " treaty like

L

Parliament was making, in hopes of good faith
from Charles; " good from this man, against
whom God hath witnessed, and whom thou
knowest!" When, therefore, the southern
army called for the King's trial, Cromwell
with the forces in the north approved. The
soldiers demanded a dissolution of Parliament,
but the Independent politicians were content
with a purge, and in December the Commons,
forcibly cleared of moderates, set up a High
Court of Justice.

Convinced by the fate of some last ap-
proaches that Charles would never make final
religious concessions, the Independent leaders
resolved at last on the course urged, for a year
past, by the rank and file. Of 135 commissioners appointed, only fifty-two appeared to
try the King; the Lords' refusal to charge
him with treason to the nation was brushed
aside. Deaf to the pleas of the Prince of
Wales and foreign powers, ignoring the objec-
tions of Fairfax and the moderates, resolutely,
and in the light of day, this small group of
fanatics tried the King for violating the
limited power entrusted to him by the people.
On the 30th January, 1649, Charles was
executed, by no known law and a nameless
executioner.

" Be not offended," wrote Cromwell later,

" at the manner of God's working; perhaps
no other way was left." Perhaps not; but
" that which you get by force is nothing."

The royal cause, thus crushed in England,
still lingered in Ireland and Scotland, mingled
in each with racial and religious forces formidable to the English army. The Irish wars
had degenerated into cross-sections of creed,
race, and barbarism, Popish Celts obeying a
papal legate, loyal Catholics, royalist Protestants, Ulster Scots, English Puritans. Charles'
gallant Deputy, Ormonde, obstructed by
Papalists and defeated by Puritans, had run
his course before Oliver landed at Dublin in
August. In two campaigns the resistance of
Catholic Ireland was broken, Cromwell showing by the massacres he allowed, at Drogheda
and Wexford, the Puritan purpose to avenge
the blood shed in 1641.

Kirk and army in Scotland were tougher
antagonists. By ejecting the " Engagers "
from their ranks, and by the execution of the
Cavalier Montrose, they proved their intention
to fight only for a Presbyterian King. Forced
to play this unfamiliar rôle, the young Charles
landed in June 1650 at Cromarty and accepted
the Covenant, and the momentous possibility
of restoration at the hands of a Scottish
Presbyterian army faced the rulers of England.

The battle of Dunbar (3rd September), pre-cipitated by the over-confidence of the Scots preachers, wiped out Leslie's army, and delivered the Lowlands into English hands. Efforts to win Scotland by negotiation, and Cromwell's illness, delayed further action till June 1651, when, determined to force a deci-sion and avoid the strain of another winter's war, he advanced on the Highlands and seized Perth. He had thereby consciously risked opening for Charles the roads to the south; the " crowning mercy " of Worcester justified his confidence, for it destroyed the last royal army and closed the wars. After forty days of wandering in disguise, Charles reached the dangerous refuge of France.

CHAPTER IX

COMMONWEALTH AND PROTECTORATE

MILITANT Royalism was thus extinguished in all three kingdoms, and it was never Royalism, pure and simple, which endangered the Puritan victory. It was, rather, the intense conservatism which had half inspired the original outbreak—the clinging to common law, order, and continuity, against things new, arbitrary, or wild, whether dictated by a King, an army, or a priesthood.

The Commonwealth , as constituted without King or Lords, represented at most the feelings of one-fifth of the nation. Defeated Royalists and Presbyterians drew together in common detestation. The rump of the Long Parliament, twice purged and emptied by death, absence, and exile, represented nothing but itself. Since 1647 the army had called for its dissolution; beyond that they were divided, for some wished a new Parliament on the old plan, others an assembly of selected saints.

If a soul can be postulated of a revolution, it survives longest in the army that saves it. The Ironsides always refused to consider themselves mere mercenaries, and in various pronouncements of 1648–9 stated "fundamentals," which alone could satisfy the good cause. Religious toleration, a legislature chosen on a wide franchise and redistributed seats, these must be raised above the whim of parliaments. The war, too, had caused many evils that demanded speedy remedy. The arteries of trade were choked; the lands seized from Crown, Church, and Cavaliers were almost exhausted; the monthly assessments and excise, which financed the army, were heavy and unpopular. The law courts ceased to function; Chancery was clogged with thousands of cases. Litigation was ruinously expensive, and obstructed by obsolete procedure. Religion was still unsettled. Extremists set up the Word of God against Presbytery, which was the law of the land, and attacked the tithe system; Parliament itself sheltered too many of the ungodly, war profiteers whose "puritanism" was reduced to coal mines borrowed from the bishopric of Durham, leases bought at knock-down prices, official salaries, and army contracts. On top of all came the fratricidal war of 1652 against

Holland, a sister republic, postponing all hopes of reform and prosperity.

The legislators showed that they meant to perpetuate themselves by co-optation, and hence, pushed on by the Independent churches, Cromwell in April 1653 forcibly evicted them. The turn of the saints had come, and with " Barebones' Parliament " (April to December) revolutionary Puritanism reached its zenith. Named by Cromwell, who as General was the one conceivably legal power surviving, on recommendations from the congregations, this body of one hundred and forty were the select men of the cause. Their measures were radical, modern, and full of lofty aspiration; they abolished imprisonment of debtors, legalised civil marriage, reinstituted parish registers. But they suffered from the reformers' malady of unconstructiveness. If they destroyed Chancery, the need for equity would find another channel; they could, as their majority wished, abolish tithes, but a preaching ministry would still have to be fed. Their internal differences were ceaseless, and finally the more Cromwellian section surrendered their powers into the General's hand.

Parliament and the saints both having failed, the army had to make a constitution, and the Council of Officers formed the " Instrument of Government " in December 1653, the first rigid type of constitution in English history. The powers of sovereignty were divided between three parties—Protector, Council of State, and a single-chamber Parliament. Security for all that the army held dear was assured by giving the sword to Protector and Council, by settling on them a fixed revenue sufficient for this and normal purposes, and most of all by making the whole Instrument, including guarantees for toleration, unalterable and fundamental. In other respects, it was an enlightened and honest scheme. Representation was diverted from rotten boroughs to counties, or to growing cities like Leeds and Manchester; the franchise was put on a uniform basis of personal wealth, which ignored tenures; members were summoned from Scotland and Ireland.

But neither neat mechanism nor real reform could close the breach between army and Parliament. The Commons, though chosen on a franchise debarring all Cavaliers, and deprived of a hundred members whom the Council prevented sitting, at once took up their historic claims. They pressed for sole financial powers, declined to except " damnable heresy " from their realm of legislation, attacked an army command which was almost autonomous, and questioned the whole Constitution. In January 1655 they were dissolved. For eighteen months the Protector returned to governing through the Council of State, reinforcing it by his " little invention " of Major-Generals, eleven of whom administered for the Council an England divided into military provinces. This period of dictatorship was ended by the needs of war finance, and in September 1656 Oliver summoned his second Parliament. This appeal to public opinion revived the feud of civilian and military. The Commons refused to renew the decimation tax on Cavaliers, which financed the Major-Generals, and asked that the army should be superseded by the constitutional force, the militia. Legal opinion, working with moderate Cromwellians, brought forward the " Humble Petition and Advice," which proposed to restore not merely civilian supremacy, but the full privileges of Parliament, an Upper House, and hereditary monarchy. The Protector himself would plainly have preferred a legal crown to this perpetual sitting upon bayonets, but weeks of conferences showed the bitter republicanism of his old companions in arms, and he concluded that Providence had

" witnessed " against kingship. The new
constitution, as finally accepted, gave him
power to name his successor and restored a
house of Peers; taken with the express
provision made for freedom of speech and
election, it made a long stride backward to the
old forms of government.

The second session of 1657-8 proved that
restoration of parliamentary liberties meant
the end of Cromwellianism. Only the upper
House now shielded army and Protector;
he filled it, therefore, with his staunchest supporters, who were replaced in the Commons
by the Presbyterians and Republicans pre-
viously excluded. Persistent attack on the
powers of the " peers " threatened, then,
government's very existence; after so many
endeavours, Oliver dissolved his last Parliament in February 1658, with a " God judge
between you and me."

He was resisting the free development of
civilian England, whence he sprang, and his
immunity from personal ambition only makes
plainer the certain doom awaiting dictatorship. Every step he had taken since Naseby
had only followed those of more dogmatic
men. Reluctantly he had led them against
Parliament, reluctantly taken supreme command from Fairfax. " God and the people,"

he claimed, had called him to this place; till they recalled that trust, he would rather be rolled into his grave with infamy than abandon it.   But even if the voice of God and the people were the same, the " people " in his sense, by 1658, were narrowed down to a few thousand redcoats.

The title of his Government was revolutionary. Its very origin, the Instrument of Government, was the work of a military committee. English legal scruple became insistent; judges began to resign, merchants to refuse tonnage and poundage. The plain fact was that the Protectorate existed on sufferance; that a free parliament meant a majority of Presbyterians, concealed Royalists, and republicans. Manufacture of borough charters, purges of Parliament, and the use of English officers to " represent " Scotland and Ireland, showed sufficiently the Government's sense of its isolation.

The opposition might be grouped in four categories, two on the right, two on the left. On the far right, and least dangerous during Oliver's life, were the Cavaliers. Their best leaders were dead, or in exile. They were financially ruined, badly led, and factious. Old men, who clung to pure Royalism and believed in waiting for inevitable reaction, hampered young men who asked for action and a Presbyterian alliance. The one rising of importance, that of 1655 in Wiltshire, was premature.

Far stronger was the Presbyterian and Independent aristocracy—nobles, squires, and lawyers. Some resented the rule of Prides, Hackers, and the rest of a new professional soldiery. Many detested the heresy of toleration; all reverenced the law and Parliament. Amongst them were the first war leaders, like Fairfax, Manchester, or Northumberland; the mass of the merchant class, weary of war and taxation; lawyers in large practice, even holding office, like the illustrious Matthew Hale. These were " the sober gentry," whom Monk later advised Richard Cromwell to humour, the necessary core of any seventeenth-century Government.

In the left centre were important disaffected Republicans. Vane, the idealist; Ludlow, a regicide who could not stomach a crowned general; Harrison, leader of the Fifth Monarchy fanatics; Haselrig, the toughest debater of the day; Lambert, a dangerous military rival. Beyond them came extremists of all coats and colours, Levellers and sectaries. With these last Oliver never attempted to compromise. He believed in

aristocracy, and shot Levellers for corrupting
the army. Liberty of religion and property
he held to be noble things, but both abused for
" the patronizing of villainies." He had little
sympathy with agitators who spoke of Saxon
freedom and Norman servitude, or with
Winstanley's " diggers," who chose Rich-
mond Hill as the first site of a communist
Eden. " Nothing but ' overturn, overturn ; ' "
" Little better than beasts,"—such were
Oliver's comments. This extreme joined in
conspiracy with the other, the Cavaliers.
Pamphlets instigated his assassination; as
fast as Thurloe, the Secretary, unravelled one
plot, another was begun. The Protector, with
a pistol in his pocket, his own life-guard
tampered with, London juries acquitting the
frothy demagogues like Lilburne who attacked him, was the supreme victim to
minority government.

This tension—a state of siege, political and
moral—could hardly have endured longer,
even had Oliver survived. There was war
without; with Holland till 1654, with Spain in
two continents, from 1655–9. Mixed motives
of morality and police suppressed the
drama, race-meetings, maypoles. Adultery
was punishable with death, and swearing with
heavy fines. A standing army of 55,000 men

policed a population of five millions. And if spiritual freedom in the wider sense was lost, religion itself was sunk in chaos. Tithes and private patronage still irregularly continued; three principal churches, Independents, Baptists, and Presbyterians, shared the parishes. Central control there was none, save in the old " Committee for plundered ministers," or fluctuating bodies of " triers " appointed by the Protector. There were many Vicars of Bray who slid from one church to another; many schemes for reunion, but no agreement.

After religion, the Puritan public wanted prosperous trade, but this, too, was lacking. Taxation was at a level undreamed of by Charles I. The " Humble Petition " settled £1,300,000 as the constant revenue, but expenditure in 1657–8 was 2½ millions. The excise, copied from Holland, was hated and resisted. Loss of the Spanish trade hit the all-important cloth industry. Royalism troubled the American plantations. Faction in London and India disturbed rival East India companies.

Half of the Commonwealth's military force was engaged in garrisoning Ireland and Scotland. From the first of these no Restoration need be feared. All England was agreed on persecution, and Cromwell's settlement was

only the logical end of Tudor policy. As it
was, the Rebellion and ensuing ten years cost
Ireland some 600,000 lives; wolves reap-
peared round Dublin; slavers took captives to
work in the Indies; trade was almost gone.
The Settlement Act of 1652 transferred about
two-thirds of the soil to some 40,000 new
owners, either " adventurers " who had lent
money in 1642 or Cromwellian soldiers, and
offered to the evicted Catholics a choice
between exile and Connaught. Over three
hundred garrisons, successively commanded by
Ireton, Ludlow, and the Protector's able son
Henry, held down this poor colony; only in
Scottish Ulster did any prosperity survive.

Presbyterianism in Scotland had not to
fear this type of conquest. They were not
Catholics and barbarians, but erring brethren :
" I beeseech you in the bowels of Christ,"
Oliver had written, " think it possible you
may be mistaken." His constant overtures
were not received by any, save a small group
of interested officials. Religion and pride in
a national monarchy forbade the Scots to
obey a heretic usurper; conspiracy was un-
ceasing, and only the presence of Monk,
with a large army, stopped it maturing into
war. Justice and prosperity were given to
Scotland, but liberty denied.

There is one glory of civil and political

liberty, there is another of the ordered heroic
State; and if freedom was stifled alike by
Strafford and Cromwell, other things must
determine our choice between two systems of
" Thorough." When ten years later the Dutch
were burning Chatham, when Louis XIV was
selecting mistresses to inspire the policy
of Charles II, Englishmen looked back to
Oliver's days, as Frenchmen of 1820 to Tilsit
and Marengo. This Government, narrow
though its basis, was rich in character and
ability. The Cromwells, Oliver and Henry,
the admirals Blake, Penn, Monk, and
Montague; Thurloe, the Secretary, with
Milton and Marvell in his office; Hale, Ashley
Cooper, Whitlocke, Lockhart—in every branch
of public service an adaptable ability, an
opening for the talents. Whatever else it
added or took away, Puritanism gave tonic
to the English mind. The Universities were
filled with new intelligence; it was in this
decade that the Royal society was born in
Wren's circle at Oxford, that the Platonist
theologians arose at Cambridge, that the
literary instinct, long obsessed with theology,
poured itself out in treatises of politics,
economics, and medicine, that the three
instruments of public opinion until the age of
Anne—the newsletter, pamphlet, and coffee-
house—first attained their strength.

Much of the Puritans' breadth of toleration, their spirit of improvement, was merged in the continued life of Restoration England; some disappeared, not wholly to be recaptured till the nineteenth century. Some illustration of their actual or projected legislation has been given; it is enough to add that it included diminution of capital punishment, abolition of copyhold, registry of land titles, cheap litigation, and other reforms which were still aspirations to the Utilitarians. Finally, strong though the front of politics was against its opponents, toleration was wider in practice than in law. A London Episcopalian could hear his service with impunity, unoffending Catholics were not persecuted, the Jews were allowed to trade and open a synagogue.

This last epoch of the English Reformation was neither inspired nor constrained by foreign influences. The Thirty Year' War turned after 1635 into a French-Swedish attack upon the Hapsburgs; it continued from 1648–59 as a duel between France and Spain, during four of which years France was crippled by the revolution of the Fronde. Neither Richelieu nor Mazarin dreamed of assisting the Stuarts, who were deprived of their last European ally in 1650 by the death of William II of Orange. The foreign policy of the Protector was almost uninfluenced by

M

internal vicissitudes, and linked up the continuous expansion of England from Elizabeth to Charles II. Religion, it is true, counted first with him. Spain was the " providential " enemy; he hoped for an Evangelical league of northern Europe; his alliance with France was conditional on a cessation of the massacre of the Vaudois. But in essentials he followed the traditional natural scheme of English alliance. Even his wish to win military points in Europe, like Dunkirk and Bremen, had Elizabethan parallels; his choice of France and Sweden for friends, his efforts at good relations with Holland and Portugal, coincided with the considered policy both of Burghley and Clarendon. The sea-war with the Dutch, terminated in 1654, was one of those tussles where neither opponent can reach the other in a vital part. England was hard-pressed financially, and her Colonies treating with the enemy; the carrying trade on which Holland depended for existence was temporarily ruined. Peace on these conditions could only be a truce. Dutch recognition of the English flag's supremacy in the narrow seas, and promises of compensation for damage in the East, broke down in unofficial feuds beyond each Government's control. English and Dutch East India companies were at each other's throats, complaints of Dutch

aggression on the fisheries, of Dutch abuse of
contraband, nearly precipitated the second
war which Charles II waged. Only mutual
fear of the two dynasties, Stuart and Orange,
bound the two republics together. Meanwhile
Spain and France each bid high for the help
of the veteran English army. Cromwell
recommended his son to read Raleigh's "History of the World;" but colonial rivalry with
Spain was not his reason for making the alliance of 1655 with Mazarin. In Spain he saw
the capital of Popery, the centre of the
Inquisition, the mistress of the vital Low
Countries, the barrier to expanded trade.
English regiments showed on the Flemish
Dunes the fighting qualities proved at Marston
Moor and Dunbar; Dunkirk and Mardyke
were won and garrisoned. But the maritime
war was haphazard and unhappy; only acci-
dent won Jamaica, the attack on the Spanish
Main was a failure.

The lasting legacy of the Protectorate was
the standing army and sea-power. Monk's
regiments and the Dunkirk garrison formed
the germ of the first; the sea commanders
and administrators—Blake, Penn, Montague,
Lawson, Vane, and Pepys—passed on to the
next Government a solid tradition of naval
organization, and a body of expert talent.
Blake drove Rupert from the Tagus to piracy

in the Indies, established the fleet in the
Mediterranean, and repressed the Algerine
corsairs. English sea-power intervened again
in 1658–9 in the Baltic to prevent a Dutch
trading monopoly and to save Sweden from
extinction.

Oliver died on the 3rd September 1658, and
his amiable eldest surviving son, Richard,
succeeded. A few months showed that the
soldiers, who made the basis of the Protectorate, had obeyed a general and not a family;
by May they were asking an army command
independent of the civil power, and compelled
Richard to dissolve his Parliament. Now
Oliver's " healing and settling " hand had
gone, the component parts of Independency
flew apart. Military " grandees " like Fleet-
wood, who had meant to keep a puppet Protector, were outbid by the preachers and the
military democracy, who now forced Richard
to resign and restored the Republic with
the Rump. This antiquated and ridiculous
survival did, after all, represent the civilian
element which had waged the war against
tyranny; with an obstinacy that was almost
magnificent, they refused to give the soldiers
sole control of military appointments, or the
religious settlement they asked. In October
the military group, led by Lambert, ejected
the Rump and set up a Committee of Safety;

revolution had reached its invariable close, a blind-alley, for no more advance was possible, and retreat could only be led by anti-revolutionaries.

The Cheshire rising, led by Sir George Booth in August, revealed the discord dividing the Royalist and Presbyterian oppositions, and the glory of overthrowing Lambert's sheer military tyranny was due to the incurably civic temper of the Puritans. Not only Monk in Scotland, but the army in Ireland and the fleet declared for Parliament, which at the Christmas of 1659–60 recovered its authority. The passion for a legal settlement, once aroused, must go far beyond the Rump, and every step taken by Monk and his associates, to provide against a return of Lambert's army, insensibly led towards the old constitution. By the time he entered London with the Scottish troops in February, it was certain that only a new, freely elected Parliament could satisfy the nation; his readmission of the members secluded in 1648, whose last service then had been the treaty of Newport with Charles I, made restoration of Charles II almost sure. In March the Rump finally declared itself dissolved; in April the Convention Parliament was elected, with that Royalist-Presbyterian majority which Cromwell had suppressed and which Monk represented.

If Monk made any restoration possible, restoration without conditions was mainly the work of Clarendon. Any specific pledges on religion, on title to land, or amnesty, must offend some section whom it was urgent to please, and conditions might be forced on Charles which would make him less than a doge of Venice. To Monk, therefore, to Fairfax, and the Puritan politicians full security was given for their personal and political reward, but the demand for limitations on the Crown and Church was met in the declaration of Breda by the formula with which Monk himself had crushed the military, " subject to the assent of a free elected Parliament." Neither logically, nor actually, could Monk now have dammed the current he had released, and before the Convention met on the 25th April he had reached agreement with the King.

At last, after twenty years of warring forces and ideals, England had recovered her *via media*. The army, which on the 29th May sullenly watched Charles' entry into London, was in truth neither more nor less the defeated party than the Crown; with a freely elected Parliament the revolution had begun; a freely elected Parliament was the victor at its close.

CHAPTER X

CHARLES II

WHAT was demonstrated in 1660 was thus
the inevitability of gradualness; what was
restored was the normal development of the
nation. Compromise was reached between
the war's two strongest combatants, Royalists
and moderate Puritans. The last time they
had co-operated was in 1641, and the constitutional work of that year now stood un-
challenged; " Thorough " was buried with
Strafford; no more was heard of Star Chamber
and ship-money. The Puritans kept the bulk
of the lands they had won during the Commonwealth; they even kept, it will be seen,
a general liberty of conscience. They had
their full share of political power. Monk,
Manchester, Morrice, Shaftesbury, sat in successive Cabinets. Scotland was ruled for
two-thirds of the reign by the Presbyterian
Lauderdale. The Hague Embassy was continued in Downing, Cromwell's American
scoutmaster; the Paris Embassy went to

Holles, one of the " five members "; Montague, now become Lord Sandwich, led a group of former Puritans in command of the fleet. Two Puritan divines accepted bishoprics; many continued in the universities.

Continuity was stamped upon the Restoration, and the best testimony to the safety of peaceful Puritans comes from the house of Cromwell. The ex-Protector Richard lived unscathed to hear the news of Blenheim and Ramillies; his sister Lady Russell to meet the first Hanoverian. Freed from the bonds of war and fanaticism, the best energy of both parties was absorbed in activities of peace. The soldiers faded into ploughmen and artizans, the intelligence dedicated to the Gospel or artillery was harnessed to commerce and literature. Pilgrim and Worldly Wiseman marched in the plain together, undivided for the time being by the high pressure of ideals.

Of this new age, Charles II was no contemptible type. If neither politically nor privately a man of principle, he was at least a man of the modern world. He realized the limitations to his prerogative, and grasped that final authority could only be wielded through the Commons. He was more genuinely tolerant than nine-tenths of his

subjects. He liked a wild day at sea as
much as Newmarket, and took a discerning
interest in commerce, the Navy, and natural
science. In the worst phases of his foreign
policy he did not lose sight of British interests,
just as in the worst company he kept the
power of distinguishing good and evil. An
ever-reinforced bevy of frail beauty squeezed
Charles Stuart for grants, lands, and diamonds,
but did not appreciably affect the King's
policy. If from his grandfather, Henry of
Navarre, he inherited this weakness, he had
a flash also of his gift of Kingship, and
bestowed more popularity on the Crown than
any sovereign between Elizabeth and Victoria.

His reign may be divided into six stages.
From his accession to the dissolution of the
Convention in January 1661, the period
winding up the revolution; the ministry of
Clarendon and the supremacy of the Cavaliers,
1661-7; the King's personal government
through the Cabal, 1667-73; Danby and the
return to the Cavaliers, 1673-8; the Popish
plot and anarchy, 1678-81; and a Royalist
reaction, lasting to the close in 1685. But
two things persist throughout, the monarchy
and public opinion; throughout we are conscious that nothing of pre-Civil-War England
has been restored, save the shell of the

constitution. The Crown and the Lords, rising
after ten years in the grave, were pale ghosts
of their old robustness. The King did,
indeed, claim the choice of ministers, control
of foreign policy, and Elizabeth's Church
supremacy; the Cavalier Parliament restored
to the Crown, on paper, its lost prerogatives,
the power of the sword, the summons and
dissolution of Parliaments, and imposed on
office-holders, soldiers, and divines, terrific
oaths of non-resistance to the established
government. But the Cavaliers, who thus
designed to ostracize Puritans as a party,
continued the work of Puritan politicians.
They severely limited the King's revenue,
denied his right to control religion by proclamation, guarded the independence of local
government against Whitehall, examined royal
accounts, and passed the Act of Habeas
Corpus. They evicted Clarendon and Danby
by impeachment, the Cabal by impeachment
and stoppage of supplies, and defied the
King's foreign and religious programme as a
whole. The clock could not be put back,
as Clarendon fondly imagined, to 1641, that
year of constitutional grace when a unanimous
Parliament had restored the balance of
executive and legislature. Since then, public
opinion had been created in a weekly Press

and incessant debate. Movements of landed property and rapid commercial growth had definitely transferred the balance of wealth from Lords to Commons. Aristocracy was still a mighty force, and was long so to continue, but it turned upon wealth, not upon the Lords as an order, whose place in the State rested henceforward, not on their constitutional powers, but on the hold of individual borough owners over the composition of the Commons.

Strong though the passions still were of Puritan and Cavalier, bitter though the memories of the scaffold, broken homes, lands lost, and evictions, the very fact that the same Cavalier Parliament between 1661 and 1678 destroyed three ministries, shows that government did not yet proceed on party lines. Cavaliers were prone to support the Court, but they also represented the " country," and there were matters—Romanism, France, and a standing army—in which a solid House of Commons would oppose the Crown. The Exclusion Parliaments should, then, be viewed as more than a Puritan, or Whig, party triumph, and the reaction of 1681 as more than a Tory revenge. In the one case the King was threatened, in the other supported, by a vehement unanimity of national feeling.

This incorporation into national life of much of the Puritan revolution extended even to the Church. The character of wholesale persecution associated with Clarendon's code is a legend—that is, if contrasted with what had gone before. Like the Presbyterians before them, the Restoration Government, driven on by their supporters, legalized a persecution which in practice was mitigated. The King's wish for tolerance was notorious; political Puritanism was still much too powerful to alienate; Cabinet ministers and many justices refused to administer the persecuting statutes; it was only at moments of political frenzy that the Conventicle or Five Mile Acts were systematically applied. The growing tolerance of Protestants towards each other, implied in the circumstances of Restoration and vital in the interests of trade, was enhanced by their growing fear of Popery, even more by that scientific rationalizing spirit, which tokened the swift approach of the eighteenth century.

Mere conservatism could not cope with these conditions, and of this Clarendon's ministry is clear proof. Our debt to his work in 1660–1 must always be acknowledged, for he did most to turn partizan reaction into national compromise. The executions clamoured for were limited to thirteen regicides, and Sir Henry Vane. The lands bought from Cavaliers, compelled to sell by the Commonwealth's crushing fines, were left in their purchasers' hands. The army was paid off and disbanded, and though Cromwellians shared in the plots and rumours that for ten years alarmed Government, the mass peacefully melted into civil life. The King's revenue was limited to £1,200,000, or less than the Protector's. Commonwealth judges were continued in office.

In all this Clarendon co-operated with the Convention. The religious settlement was more embarrassing. Episcopacy, hallowed by the death of Charles I and Laud, was bound to return; the surviving bishops of old days, like Juxon, were few, and the Churchmen's new leader was Sheldon, archbishop from 1663. Their policy was the clean slate; to wipe out the Commonwealth's work as usurpation, and restore the old establishment in every detail. Politically, this was out of the question. The King was a sceptic, leaning to Romanism as the best faith for monarchy; Clarendon a firm Anglican, but pledged to conciliation and fearful of renewing civil troubles. There is no reason to view as insincere the royal Declaration issued in

October 1660, which associated presbyters with bishops in ordination, and lightened the terms of subscription to the Articles. For it was accompanied by offers of bishoprics and deaneries to leading Dissenters and expressly declared to be provisional, in accordance with the pledge given at Breda, that final settlement should be left to Parliament.

In 1661-2 the whole Cavalier interest in the Commons made it clear that they would resist the King's concession. At the Savoy Conference the bishops refused to budge from their legal vantage-ground; by the Act of Uniformity the Commons proposed to expel all ministers not episcopally ordained. All amendments suggested by the King and Clarendon were rejected, and the first attempt in 1663, to give toleration by the prerogative had to be withdrawn before the Commons' wrath. The eviction of two thousand ministers was not followed by the disturbances Government had feared; the passing of the Conventicle, Corporation, and Five Mile Acts, completed the Commons' scheme for driving Puritans out of office, for suppressing their meetings, and depriving them of their preachers. But the passive resistance, which checked this persecution in practice, was winked at by the Crown, and Clarendon's fall was brought about not by injured Puritans, but by King and Commons.

The Chancellor was an Elizabethan, prolonged into a new and naughty world. He believed in a balance of Crown and law; he would neither be a royal slave nor a parliamentary minister; if King and Parliament disagreed, somewhere in the books of the Inner Temple a solution could be found. The Council, composed of the great officers of state, should assist the King to govern; it was for them to execute the King's will (whether they agreed with it, or not), when it did not conflict with the law. The four hundred country gentlemen in the Commons had the sole right of voting taxes and making laws, but were not concerned with policy. From such a view of government, in the conditions after 1660, two results followed; bad administration, and quarrels with the legislature. The Council board was too cumbrous to control the specialized functions involved by modern war and finance; the Commons' voice created the money credit on which administration now depended, and could not be prevented from calling administration to account. Other reasons contributed, more creditable to Clarendon—the hatred of Lady Castlemaine, or Charles' weariness of business

—but essentially he fell, because he ignored what even Charles saw could be ignored no longer, that the Commons were the spring of government.

The Cabal that replaced him included three men of first-rate ability: Arlington, the real minister for foreign affairs; Lauderdale, the despot of Scotland; and Shaftesbury, who was a power with the Commons and city. It was completed by the vicious, flashy Buckingham, whose Puritan marriage to a Fairfax was offset by sharing in Charles' lowest vices, and Clifford, a blustering Catholic Cavalier. If Clarendon outraged the Commons by his method of government, the Cabal collided with them on policy, and their fall is the clearest example of the King's ultimate subjection to Parliament. A Cabinet in the modern sense they were not, for personal struggles divided them, and in their one point of agreement, religious toleration, they differed from the Parliament through whom they had to govern. Their early efforts for religious comprehension were, therefore, promptly quashed, but a wider cause explains the collapse of 1673, their association in a scheme that included toleration for Catholics by the prerogative, and alliance with France for the ruin of Holland. In this, in the proroguing of Parliament for two years, and in a stop on the Exchequer amounting to part repudiation of the national debt, all the ministers shared, but to two only, Clifford and Arlington, has been attributed the deeper guilt of connivance in a plot of the two Kings, for making a Catholic despotism in England through French arms. The sincerity of the King's brother, the Duke of York, and of Clifford in this may be accepted; that of Charles and Arlington is more obscure. Both were men of cold intelligence who, if Catholics, never practised their faith, and whatever Charles' approval of Catholicism, he never at other times showed a tendency to risk the main chance; Arlington's foreign policy as a whole was balanced, unmoral, but not Francophil. Careful examination of the secret treaty of Dover suggests that ample supplies of French money was what King and minister most desired; much earlier, poverty had driven Charles to beg loans from half the Powers of Europe, while schemes for military assistance in case of rebellion constantly figured in his negotiations. But, whatever the precise degree of guilt in the actors of the moment, the simultaneous declarations of war upon Holland and of Indulgence for all Dissenters defied both nation and consti-

N

tution, and when Parliament, early in 1673, was permitted to meet, it demolished these ministers. The passing of the Test Act drove York and Clifford to resign; Arlington quickly withdrew from the French alliance, and soon retreated in comfort as Lord Chamberlain; Shaftesbury made his peace with the Opposition. The Treaty of Westminster (February 1674) ended the English share in the war. Charles called on Danby and other Cavalier officials to save him from their friends and form a ministry.

Danby and Shaftesbury were the first party leaders. The first, by distribution of places, propaganda, choice of candidates, and bribery, built up a majority of Cavaliers, soon, when the Popish plot arose, to be styled Tories. Shaftesbury found a nucleus in the few remaining Puritans, like Marvell; adding to them any members he could detach from the "country" or middle group in Parliament, he created the Whigs, on a platform of no Popery, no pensionary Parliament, and no standing army.

Placating his Cavalier majority by repression of Nonconformity, Danby kept the royal favour by successful finance, and his hope was to combine King and Commons in war against France. But the conditions which at the

close of 1678 caused his downfall show the
difficulties of a minister in transition between
despotism and parliamentary monarchy. The
parliamentary influence of the King, of the
Duke (since his second marriage, to Mary
of Modena, more fanatically Catholic), and
even that of subjects like Arlington and
Lauderdale, was still independent of the first
Minister, whose tenure of office involved a
precarious balancing of such personal forces
with his own following in the Commons.
Without clear parliamentary support he could
not get Charles to make war, but war meant
a standing army, which Parliament suspected
would be used to establish Popery. Refused
money by Parliament, the King would fall
back on France; hence the secret treaties of
1677–8 with Louis XIV, which Charles ordered
Danby to sign. An unholy alliance of Louis, his
envoy at London, the English ambassador at
Paris and the Whigs, sufficed, with the Popish
plot, to destroy the one minister of Charles II
who nearly achieved a Protestant war.

The Plot gave the Whigs a chance, which
they so misused as temporarily to destroy
their party; for this they had to thank
Shaftesbury, whose brilliant political brain
now descended to crime. No party had long
retained his hectic ambition. He had fought

for both King and Parliament; since then he had been a Cromwellian peer, a minister under Clarendon, Chancellor in the Cabal, leader of Opposition to Danby. He had no religious bias, genuinely disliked persecution, and appreciated the best interests of trade. But, having once been ready to enforce toleration through the prerogative, he now planned the exclusion of York from the throne by perjury and violence. The Plot had, indeed, within it a substratum of truth, for the Jesuits had far-reaching notions of foreign assistance; but this could not excuse the use made of the " revelations " of Oates, Dangerfield, and other villains, to madden the people against all, guilty or innocent, who opposed the Whig majority in the Commons. From eviction of members, deprivation of judges, imprisonment of juries, they proceeded to attack the Queen, to proclaim the bastard Monmouth heir apparent, to organize the London mob, to attempt extension of " No Popery " to Ireland; and last, in 1682-3, to conspiracy for armed rebellion and the murder of the King. Proposals to limit, not wholly exclude, a Catholic successor, were rejected by three successive houses of Commons, and in 1681 the country was drifting into renewed civil war.

From this it was saved mainly by Charles'
courage and tenacious judgment, which allowed
violence to go on till it drove to his side all
moderate opinion, headed by the eloquent
" trimmer " Halifax. Using the same infamous weapons as Shaftesbury—packed juries,
lying informers, and a poisoned press—he
raised, none the less, a genuine Royalist
revival. The Whig excesses reaped their
nemesis in creating the Tories; the Church
of England men Charles had so often offended
rejoined him in 1681 as the sole hope of
order against rebellion. From this date till
his death, he called no Parliament. He
divided his counsels between high-church
loyalists like the younger Hydes, trimmers
like Halifax, and officials like Sunderland and
Godolphin. Relapsing into his constitutional
indolence, he sank into political negation;
French money saved him from Parliament,
even if France were conquering the world;
strong in the new loyalty of his people, he
would not again tempt the deluge. His
brother's title was accepted; Monmouth was
in exile; Shaftesbury died at Amsterdam.
Yet a King, who had spent life in learning
from events and his own errors, could not
have ignored the French threat indefinitely,
nor indefinitely have dispensed with Parlia-

ment. Had he lived ten years, had he had a legitimate son, pressure of facts must once more have induced an understanding with his people; William III might never have reigned, Lord Macaulay's " History " have never been written.

It was lack of money and fear of internal sedition which first made Charles enter the gilded cage into which Louis XIV shepherded half the princes of Europe. But a subsidy is not the same as a dole; and not till his last years did Charles lose all English inspiration. National tradition triumphed over the prejudices acquired in exile, and friendship with France and Sweden, a settlement (even by war) with Holland, alliance with Portugal, were all inherited from Thurloe and Monk. Till 1670 at least the King's wish, on urgent financial grounds, was to avoid war. The sale of Dunkirk, on these grounds so desirable, and for strategical reasons approved by experts, was a further irritation to Spain, who grudged the loss of Jamaica and the Portuguese marriage. But English diplomacy was directed to closing the Spanish-Portuguese war, and would nurse both these nations against the menacing union of France and Holland. For by 1664 Louis' ambitions on the Spanish succession were declared, and a

Franco-Dutch partition of Belgium and Spanish trade was the nightmare haunting English ministers, which explains half the diplomatic vicissitudes of the reign.

The war with Holland, of 1664–7, was an episode external to this vital and delicate balance. Disliked by Charles and Clarendon, it was pushed on by powerful sections of the nation—by York and the seamen, by the East India and African Companies, by New England interests, and by diplomats of the Cromwellian school, who believed in *Delenda est Carthago ;* to this, Charles' displeasure with the Dutch republicans, who excluded his ward, the young Orange, was entirely subordinate. Administrative corruption, parliamentary distrust, and unexpected disasters in the Plague and Fire of London, damaged the fighting qualities of the English fleet; the war closed with the scandal of the Dutch seizure of the Medway and the capital's outer defences. After three years of expensive and indecisive fighting, the peace of Breda (August 1667) established peace upon the *status quo* then existing; the net result for Britain being the addition of New York and New Jersey to her American colonies.

Of greater prospective importance was Louis XIV's attack in the same year upon

Flanders, followed by the Triple Alliance of January 1668 between England, Holland and Sweden, which forced him momentarily to be content with fortresses instead of provinces. But this alliance, glorified in retrospect as the beginning of opposition to France by the literary skill of William Temple its negotiator, must be reduced to its true perspective. Both Arlington and De Witt were waiting on events; England and Holland profoundly distrusted each other, but alike feared French aggression. Both made proposals for Belgian partition to France; both treated at Vienna and Madrid for an anti-French league. Arlington, with his Dutch wife, his Spanish training, and his linguistic gifts, was tactically one of the ablest of English foreign ministers, and the broad lines of his policy were ruled by more certain and creditable motives than truckling to Popery and despotism. Spanish bankruptcy, Austrian preoccupation with the Turks, and English poverty, really ship-wrecked the formation of any coalition against France; that being so, and France being decided to attack Holland as the next step towards the Spanish Netherlands, Charles and Arlington made bid for a share in the French gains. This policy, unmoral but not unskilful, and more akin to Bolingbroke than to James II, explains clauses in the secret negotiations of 1669–71, for the English acquisition of Sluys and Walcheren, of Ostend, Minorca, and Spanish America.

In 1673 Charles was compelled by Parliament to abandon a game which had misconceived both the English temper and the French power, and Danby returned to the anti-French policy of his friend Temple. His understanding with William of Orange, to make Charles join a European coalition, culminated in 1677 with William's marriage to James' daughter Mary, but the mutual distrust of King and Parliament destroyed the alliance, and Danby with it. For the next four years the Popish plot realized Louis' ideal, of an England crippled by internal disorder; for four more years again, Charles allowed France to master Europe by refusing to meet his Parliament.

Titles of affection, *pater patriae* and the like, are given to rulers who confer, or coincide with, an increased material wealth, and the England of Charles II was rich while the Crown was poor. Commerce had become the director of national policy. The City, great moneyed men like the Childs, Papillons, or Houblons, the East India Company, were powers comparable to the legislature; the modern minister like Danby, or courtier like John Churchill, was deep in financial speculation. The Turkey company was charged with English interests in the Levant, and appointed the minister to the Porte. Much English capital was sunk in Mediterranean ports—Tangier, Aleppo, Alicante, and Leghorn; English consuls in all trading centres represented to the Secretary of State the effects of hostile tariffs, or new openings for English goods. The Customs revenue, which in 1604 had been estimated at £130,000, brought in over £500,000 in Charles' later years, and between Restoration and Revolution English shipbuilding was doubled.

The policy which protected this wealth was one of elastic and enlightened mercantilism. Export of bullion and the open door meant profits in the East, and from mere accumulation of treasure economists turned to watch the whole balance of national trade. Regulated and joint-stock companies were still the chief agency of commerce, but their monopoly was steadily being sapped by the pressure of interlopers seeking a free trade. But the outstanding feature of Restoration policy was that the Crown, for the first time, made colonial development the first charge on its resources, and welded the plantations and factories, scattered over the globe by individuals and corporations, into something like an empire.

Charles I's flabby government had left Virginia, New England, and the West Indies to drift and separate at pleasure. The first effort at cohesion came with the Commonwealth, which included many men of colonial experience, and with the Navigation Act of 1651 bound the Colonies materially to the mother country. Charles II's ministers carried on these beginnings with greater energy. The effects of the Navigation Acts as a weapon against Holland are doubtful, but at least they consolidated the British monopoly in the plantations, and yet left freedom to the colonists in many staple trades. English dominion expanded rapidly on the north American seaboard. Charters to Rhode Island and Connecticut restricted mutinous Massachusetts; New York, New Jersey, and Delaware were won from the Dutch; Shaftesbury developed Carolina; Penn founded Pennsylvania; the Hudson's Bay Company opened up Rupert's Land and the far north; Surinam and Acadia were given up to Holland and France, but the consolidation of Jamaica, Newfoundland, Barbadoes, and the Leeward Islands more than made up this loss. Future controversies—the validity and enforcement of the Navigation dues, and every claim of autonomy—were already heard, but in the Colonies as a whole self-government on the English model, local legislatures, and self-taxation, steadily matured. Fresh fields were opened by the acquisition of Tangier (abandoned in 1684) and Bombay, as part of the Queen's dowry, and by the African company's conquests on the Gold Coast. In spite of corruption and mercantile selfishness, Charles' colonial policy was perhaps the best branch of his government. He revived in various shapes his father's Committees for Trade and Plantations, in which some of the acutest men of the age, like Shaftesbury, Locke, or Evelyn, took a leading part; an unexpected amount of religious tolerance and constitutional breadth characterized their proceedings and the colonial charters. Colonial governors were often able, independent, and vigorous; an interest, financial, intellectual, or fashionable, in overseas ventures was almost universal in Restoration politicians.

In England the ruling class, who had defeated the central government in the Civil War, had no intention of suffering continuance of the Tudors' incessant paternal interference. Careful to avoid any taxation of land and to guard themselves by tariffs from Irish competition, henceforward they passively resisted, or ignored, all attempts made to regulate prices, wages, or the taking of interest. The liberty aimed at and secured by the Puritans had begun with local self-government, and a long period now opened of absolute non-interference from Whitehall, whether with industrial relations or with the Justices' government in Quarter Sessions. New industries imported by Huguenots and other immigrants, the expansion of navigation and commerce, the survival of many yeoman farmers, and the close association of domestic industry with agriculture, all this checked, until late in the century, the harsher side of the new capitalism, and many local schemes were set on foot for the assistance of the poor. But the efforts of the legislature may be measured by the Act of Settlement (1662) which, preventing the mobility of labour in the supposed interests of London and the rich, kept poorer districts in their poverty. Increasing fluctuations of trade, a steady rate of enclosure, and the clear growth of a half-barbarous and neglected urban proletariate, were dire omens for the future.

The harm that could be done by the English aristocracy was proved in Ireland, which only the Crown saved for the moment from the final enslavement brought about by Parliament in 1688. Acceptance of Cromwell's land settlement, even in slightly mellowed form, followed inevitably from English prejudice, but under Ormonde, Lord Deputy for most of the reign, Ireland enjoyed her last period of fair social and religious tolerance for a century. The worst feature, the commercial code that banned her export trades and her woollen industry, was passed by Shaftesbury and the English Commons against protests from Ormonde and Clarendon; only the royal government, too, stopped Shaftesbury's black project of a " Popish plot," to which Archbishop Plunket, Catholic primate of Ireland, fell an innocent victim. But the respite was to be short. Violence of extreme Catholics, rancour of Ulster, and English prejudice were currents which no personal influence could long arrest.

If Irishmen may think kindly of Charles, his Scottish government was infamous. The solid constitutional opinion, which checked him in England, here did not exist; feuds of Highlanders, moderate Presbyterians, and Covenanters, blended of old hereditary and moral hatreds, made possible the full scheme of *divide et impera*. Stuart detestation of

Presbytery was deepened in Charles by the handling he had received from the Kirk in 1650, and the execution of Argyle, its lay leader, signified his decision to fight it. The Scottish Parliament, in furious anti-Cromwellian reaction, swept away the whole work accomplished since 1633, and restored Episcopacy; between 1663 and 1679 sole power was committed to Lauderdale, nominally a Presbyterian, but in fact an ideal agent of Oriental despotism. Failing to conciliate Presbytery, he set out to crush it by savage punishment; jealous of all restraint, he alienated or drove into exile the best of the nobility. Scotland's open sympathy with the Dutch and with the English opposition instigated further repression, and a standing army, sole royal control of the Church, and a declaration of indulgence were sanctioned by a packed legislature. Rebellion in 1679 was put down by Englishmen and Highlanders; for the remainder of the reign the Duke of York, whom England would not stomach, rehearsed in Scotland the pains and penalties which England was soon to endure. The policy which drove Mary Queen of Scots into England thus returned upon Scotland a century later; her fate might have suggested that it is easier to uproot a sovereign than a nationality.

Charles II, who had successfully avoided repetition of all such travels, died on the 6th February, 1685, leaving a secure and popular throne to the brother whose title he had saved, and whose stupidity he deplored. Whatever his moral failings (and infidelity to a wife is better than her execution), whatever the degree of his despotism (and subsidy treaties may be less disastrous than wasteful wars), it is at least certain that in his time England bounded forward in intelligence and power. The throne would rest henceforward upon public opinion, the Commons were the vital power in the State, the political harvest of Puritanism was safely garnered, trade and industry greatly advanced, the Empire recognized and intelligently administered. Cynicism and weariness had aided science and ideal; by the close of the reign, religious persecution for its own sake was unthinkable to most men of all parties. Not with energy, not from high motives, but with a certain intelligent foresight, Charles had sometimes indicated, more often allowed his people to follow, the avenues that led to harmony and empire.

CHAPTER XI

JAMES II AND THE FALL OF THE MONARCHY

THE throne of Elizabeth and of Charles I, for which the Cecils, Strafford, and Clarendon had laboured, was to end on a wretched ante-climax, and expire in the remarkable stupidity of James II, the venality of Sunderland, the treachery of Churchill, and the nasty mind of the Princess Anne. Such errors or weakness in the chief actors may obscure the fact that something like revolution was inevitable.

The loyal reaction of 1681–1685 was much too loyal to be true. Experienced Tories like Ormonde and Danby, and trimmers like Halifax, did not believe in the permanence of unparliamentary Kingship vassalized to France; moderate men like the diarist Evelyn were nauseated by sycophants like Judge Jeffreys, or the royal press-agent L'Estrange. The extreme Whigs, indeed, had for the moment ruined their whole party, but the Whig tradition was not buried in Shaftesbury's grave at Wimborne; revenge for the

death of Russell, Sidney, and Essex could yet
rouse hundreds, and desire for revival of
parliamentary liberties stir thousands more.
Sooner or later Louis XIV would come to
grips again with the European coalition, and
the choice be presented to England of siding
in earnest with Protestantism or anti-Christ.
Sooner or later Parliament must be recalled.

Nor could the constitution of 1660 survive
unchanged for another generation. Despite
all theories of passive obedience, Parliament
had already questioned the remaining prerogatives which Charles so obstinately guarded
—his discretionary supremacy over the Church,
his control of foreign affairs, the sole command
of the army. The Tory Danby's wish to
attack France, the practical refusal of the
ruling class to execute laws against Protestant
Dissenters, the loathing of Roman Catholicism,
proved by the Plot, and the penetration of the
Church by liberal thought, were all signs that
the " divine " authority of Church and King
were being limited. It was reserved for King
James (as three centuries earlier for Richard
II) to defy the new order, and so to make short
and sharp that revolution which would otherwise have come about by the steady erosion
of time, or through the cynical ability of King
Charles.

James was now in his fifty-second year, and had lived through the Civil War, the crisis of 1673, and the Plot without deriving any lesson save this, that only " firmness " could save government. His father, he thought, could have saved his head, his brother have crushed Holland, Catholicized England, and resisted Shaftesbury, had they only been " firm." Handed now in acclamation to the throne by a people sickened of mob-rule and conspiracy, he promised himself to carry through the firm policy he had preached, in and out of season, since his conversion in 1668—Catholicism and unrestricted royal authority. In private life he shared, in a dull, sordid way, in his predecessor's vices, but in quality as a public man he was much inferior. Long tenure of the Admiralty and Cabinet experience had given him love of the Navy and some habits of business, but he was bigoted beyond belief, implacable to enemies, and transparently disingenuous. On all questions of State except religion he vacillated perpetually, and in the crisis of the Revolution succumbed in a total nervous collapse, which only premature physical decay can excuse. The Stuart blood was, in fact, running thin, and of James' fifteen legitimate children eleven died in infancy.

Deluded by the atmosphere of the last four years, and convinced that others would, like himself, find the step short from Canterbury to Rome, James resolved first to attempt realization of his Catholic scheme through the channel of the Cavaliers. He placed their leaders, the Hydes, at the head of his ministry; Rochester, the younger but abler brother, became Treasurer, Clarendon Deputy of Ireland, their kinsman, Queensberry, Treasurer in Scotland. Of other prominent ministers, Halifax was removed to the honorific office of Lord President; Sunderland and Godolphin had both supported Exclusion, but could be counted upon to follow any `ascendant policy. It will be noticed that the staunch Protestant Tory, Danby, was not included. A few preliminary severities, such as the whipping of Oates and the imprisonment of Baxter, the Dissenting leader, whetted the loyalty of extreme Tories, and the Court pressure used in the elections during May was hardly necessary to return a Tory House of Commons. They had scarcely voted James for life the revenues enjoyed by his brother when news came which redoubled their ardour; Argyle had landed in the Highlands, and Monmouth at Lyme Regis. Argyle's expedition, rent by faction among the leaders and opposed by all the enemies of the Campbells, fell at the first blow; the failure of Monmouth is more significant.

It was not the beacon fire of 1688, but the last embers of Puritanism and the Exclusion plots. The aristocracy took up arms against Shaftesbury's pretender; Churchill, and countless others who fought James three years later, were still on his side. Orange had tried to stop Monmouth sailing, and sent the British troops in Holland to help the King. Only some surviving Cromwellians, some of Shaftesbury's Londoners, and staunch Puritans of Dorset and Somerset marched to the brief tragedy of Sedgemoor, where on the 6th July Feversham and the royal army cut them to pieces. The execution, nine days later, of " King Monmouth " raised not a ripple in political England. The King, with full national support, had crushed two rebellions within six months of his accession, and there seems little doubt but that wisdom and moderation would have enabled him to win every legitimate freedom for Catholics. But he asked for more than freedom, and of wisdom or moderation he was devoid.

Judge Jeffreys was sent to the West country, and over three hundred victims perished in the shambles of the " Bloody

Assize "; hundreds more were shipped to the Indies, or sold like cattle to courtiers and maids of honour. Cruel sentences on London Dissenters goaded Whigs to desperation, and shocked all men of humanity. James' approbation was marked by the elevation of drunken Jeffreys to the Cabinet, while the chief planks of the forthcoming session were signified by the dismissal of Halifax for resisting repeal of Habeas Corpus and the Test Act. Already the royal pledge to maintain the English Church was shamelessly violated. The King required his ministers to attend the Mass. A Papal nuncio was received in London, which was filled with Huguenots expelled from France by the revocation of the Edict of Nantes. Commissions in the army had been given to Catholics, and these faithful officers, James announced, he meant to retain.

Eleven days of November were enough to settle the religious question, so far as the Tory Parliament was concerned. They were asked to vote £1,200,000 for a standing army officered by Catholics; they offered £700,000, preferred the militia to an undisciplined and illegal army, and refused outright to repeal the Test. On the 20th November they were prorogued, not to meet again. Separated from his natural supporters, James moved on in the policy of " firmness " alone.

Not only Protestant England but Catholic
Europe (excepting the interested instigator,
Louis XIV) viewed " firmness " with dismay.
English Catholics, mostly loyal Tories and still
numerous, only asked freedom of worship.
That great Pope, Innocent XI, advised caution ; lawlessness could only bring nemesis, and
he was outraged by French tyranny in Europe
and the servitude of the French Church.   Of
the English ministers, only the heart of
Sunderland (or more accurately, the brain) was
in the business ; he was ready to outbid his
rival Rochester, even at the price of national
safety.   With him were associated the Queen,
Mary of Modena, who had lost five children,
but was still young, and passionately devoted
to husband and Church ; the Jesuit father,
Petre ; the Catholic Tyrconnel, so long the
evil spirit of Ireland.   This was the junto who
now usurped the influence lost by Rochester,
and under such auspices James proceeded to
apply the policy of Mary Tudor, without a
tithe of her constitutionalism, and after a
lapse of a hundred and thirty years.

At first, he still hoped that the bulk of the
" loyal " party would come to heel ; he would
assist the process by the full straining of his
prerogative, and weaken resistance by in-
stalling a body of Papists in power.   Like his
father, he appealed to the judges against the

law, and packed the bench. By the test case of Godden *v.* Hales, he got a verdict that he could dispense with Acts of Parliament and, on the strength of this, placed Catholics in the Council and at the head of Oxford colleges. In July 1686 he set up an Ecclesiastical Commission, defying acts of 1641 and 1661 that had condemned all such courts. On Hounslow Heath he formed a standing camp of some 16,000 men, and the Mass was celebrated in their tents. The long business began of combing out Protestants from the army and commission of the peace. He committed the Scottish Council and Edinburgh Castle to Catholics; Tyrconnel became General in Ireland. Jesuits, whose very presence in England was illegal, worked openly in London chapels and schools. Lord Castlemaine's mission to Rome violated both English law and public decency; yet it failed in its main object, for the Pope refused to crown a hopeless policy by a cardinal's hat for the aspiring Petre.

In 1687, despairing of the Tory Churchmen, James turned towards the Protestant Dissenters, whom he had harried for twenty years in England and Scotland. If he could win them by the prospect of repealing the " Clarendon " code and the Test, he might make a parliamentary coalition of Dissenters, Catholics and courtiers. The Hydes' dismissal in January marked the new method. The new Deputy was naturally Tyrconnel, who spoke openly of repealing the Settlement of 1662, the foundation of Protestant ascendancy on Irish soil. The Treasury vacated by Rochester was shared among five commissioners, of whom two were Catholics and one Godolphin. Purging was redoubled in central and local government; in countless personal interviews James pruned away his best adherents and his oldest friends. He displaced Admiral Herbert (who was to pilot the Dutch fleet in 1688) in favour of the Catholic Strickland. For London aldermen who had borne the brunt against Shaftesbury, he substituted violent Whig fanatics. In February, a declaration of Indulgence freed all Dissenters in Scotland from the penal laws; in April this was extended to England. At the same time James showed that he meant to cut the English Church at its roots, bidding the fellows of Magdalen elect a Catholic convert as President. Cambridge was tampered with in the same way; the two seminaries of the Anglican clergy were to be destroyed. Having thus forced illegality on court, army, Church, and corporate bodies, James dissolved the Parliament, so long suspended, and turned to prepare the constituencies for its successor.

A committee of councillors began to " regulate " the boroughs; Lords-Lieutenant were ordered to sound every justice of the peace. The greatest magnates in England refused, like Derby, Oxford, or Shrewsbury; they were replaced by officials like Jeffreys or by avowed Papists. Nine-tenths of the justices would not pledge themselves to repeal the Test, or assist candidates so inclined, and these obsolete Tories were replaced by Dissenters. In August and September James progressed to Worcester, Chester, and Oxford, to countenance by his presence the new coalition; he heard Mass in public, greeted Dissenters warmly, and heaped reproaches on the false " Church of England loyalty." In spite of all disappointments, he did not mean to yield; if men resisted him, a beam of approval shone from heaven, for in December it was made public that the Queen was with child.

But James was old for his years; even if the male heir, so confidently predicted among Catholics, were born, there must almost certainly be a minority. Whether the child lived or died, the matter of succession or Regency must be settled. The present heir was Mary, Princess of Orange—staunchest of

Protestants herself, and in politics a mild, faithful reflection of her husband. It was the Prince whom English statesmen looked to as the real successor; his position as the inspiring centre against France made the condition of England a question for Europe. No coalition could prosper without including Holland; but Holland, with memories of 1672 in mind, could not attack France if England were French, hardly if England were neutral. From 1686 onwards everything tokened the approach of war. Since the Peace of Nimwegen in 1678, Louis' career had been one long aggression. By " reunions " in Alsace-Lorraine, he threatened the Empire. Through the person of Madame, wife of the Dauphin, he was staking out claims in the Palatinate. Cardinal Furstenburg, so long his agent in seducing German princes, was successor designate to the Electorate of Cologne, and since the Elector held the sees of Munster and Liege also, the military keys of Germany might any day be in French hands. German national feeling was aroused. The middle party, who had long vacillated, broke away from France and in 1686 formed the league of Augsburg with Austria. Protestants, among them specially Brandenburg, were furious at the sufferings of the Huguenots; Catholics

could count upon the moral support of Rome,
which would try to avenge in Cologne the
wrongs Louis had inflicted in France and
Italy.

But Louis' most brutal aggressions were
never aimless, and the problem to which he
had dedicated his life—the Spanish succession
—was coming to a head. At the moment his
chances seemed unfavourable. So far as the
Spanish Court could be committed, it was so
now to the claims of the Electress of Bavaria,
daughter of the Emperor Leopold by his first
Spanish wife. Much as Leopold would have
preferred to sacrifice his daughter to his sons
by a second marriage, he was anyhow decided
to fight a French succession. Soon he could
hope to be freed from his long Turkish warfare,
soon he could lead his army to the Rhine or
Pyrenees. The breach was therefore imminent; 'twere not well, some of Louis' advisers
argued, that it came quickly? Let him
anticipate the Austrians, and master Germany
before dealing with Spain.

But while the eyes of Orange were turned to
the Turks at Buda-Pesth, or to the morbid
intrigues of Madrid, James II was pressing
his "firm" policy on England. He had a sort
of patriotism, was proud of the ships he had
once led, and once had been ready to fight

France. But now he could think of nothing but the faith; for that, peace abroad was absolutely vital, for war would mean a Protestant Parliament. He would take no side in Europe. True, in 1685 he asked and obtained some French money, and refused to protest against their suppression of the Huguenots; but to active measures, to alliance with France, neither Louis nor his experienced ambassador Barillon could ever persuade him. This flickering spark of independence irritated the French, who finally abandoned a King on whom they could not depend. Still, for most of the reign, it was enough for France that King and Parliament were at daggers-drawn; it meant that England was a nullity in Europe, and that Louis could safely stop the pension which the more dangerous Charles had exacted.

Facts thus did not justify the Dutch conviction that England and France were bound by secret treaty, but in religion Louis had a weapon which gave an appearance of truth to this suspicion. Convinced from France that William was making an offensive Protestant alliance, James turned a deaf ear to the Dutch in every controversy, whether in the French seizure of Orange, the immunity given by Holland to British exiles like Burnet, or the

command of British troops in Dutch service.
Moreover, William could not be passive where
England was concerned.   It was rumoured
that James meant to press Catholicism on his
second daughter Anne and her husband, and
give them priority in the succession : even his
failure would for William be nearly as disastrous as his success, for civil turmoil in
England might result in a Commonwealth.
On all grounds, then, he must achieve an
understanding with the English; with the
King, if possible, for the Crown's support was
valuable in his struggle with the burghers of
Amsterdam; if not, with the Opposition.
Already, the Prussian Elector advised him to
invade England; already Louis' minister at
the Hague had predicted this must come.

James, who had himself so narrowly
escaped exclusion, had no wish originally to
exclude Mary and William.   He loved his
daughters, and was anxious to secure his
infant Catholicism by agreement with his
heirs, who might later have power to uproot
it; the Opposition, who since 1680 had de-
ferred to William's judgment, were eager for
it now.   These conditions attach great importance to the mission of Dykvelt, William's
envoy, early in 1687.   To James the message
was, that the Prince and Princess, though

willing to give toleration, could in no circumstances agree to repeal the Test; not even for the reward of alliance against France. From Rochester and Danby, Halifax and Nottingham, Shrewsbury and Churchill, the envoy carried back messages of devotion; they did not (save perhaps Danby) speak yet of resistance, but let it be understood they were ready to join Orange in any remedy he proposed.

By the spring of 1688 the English were more pronounced. Some, like the wary Halifax, advised William that James made no progress; that his projected Parliament would never materialize, and that he would hang himself if given enough rope. But the more active—Danby, Shrewsbury, and Russell— feared that the people would hang before the King. "Regulators," selected sheriffs, new justices, might pack a House of Commons; new peers might flood the Lords; army and navy were being watered with Papists, and what legend said Strafford had tried with one Irish army, Tyrconnel might, in truth, accomplish with another. In April, therefore, they sent Russell over to ask when William could be ready to invade England.

The international situation was more critical than ever. Exasperated by William's firm-

ness, James in January demanded the return
of the British battalions from Holland. On
refusal, he began to prepare a fleet, and
negotiated with France for assistance. The
prospect of a British-French alliance, in
defence of a Catholic settlement, roused the
Dutch Calvinists, and finally converted them
to William's scheme. In agreement with the
States-general's leaders, he replied to the
English rebels that, if invited by " the most
valued " in the nation, he could be ready by
late September. It will be noted that invasion was arranged before the trial of the
seven bishops, or the birth of the Prince of
Wales.

But only these two last events determined
the character of the Revolution, turning it
from precarious rebellion or invasion into a
national defection from the Crown. The
second declaration of Indulgence was issued
in April; in May the clergy were bidden to
read it in their churches. The refusal of
Sancroft and his suffragans to obey united the
country. Since five of the seven bishops were
later Non-Jurors who refused to acknowledge
William's title, it will be seen with what an
effort the party of Divine right nerved itself
to resist the Lord's anointed; as it was, by
putting the bishops in the dock on a charge

of seditious libel, James finally destroyed passive obedience, and tore the Church apart from the Crown. Nor, in so doing, had he won the Dissenters, whose best leaders rejected his offers, and made plain their sympathy with the Churchmen. Neither the cheers of the royal troops, nor rejoicings in every village at the bishops' acquittal, stopped James; was he not (since the 10th June) father of a Prince of Wales? He continued to introduce Irish soldiers, dismissed two judges who had voted for the acquittal, and summoned the long-matured Parliament for November. When at last in mid-September he tried to turn back, he was months too late.

Side by side the English revolution and the European war rolled towards the brink, where they were to meet and surge over together. Popular disbelief in the genuineness of the new prince was general, but this was not the determining factor with the aristocracy who conducted this revolution. The final invitation to Orange, dated the 30th June, was signed by four Whigs (Shrewsbury, Devonshire, Henry Sidney, and Russell) and by three Tories (Danby, Bishop Compton of London, and Lumley). Before summer was over, they won the adherence of Anne and her husband,

P

of soldiers like Churchill, Trelawny, and Kirke; of magnates like Ormonde, Bath, and Lowther; of Charles II's son Grafton, and of two among the seven bishops. In September English nobles and gentry were gathering at the Hague: at home, court, army, and fleet were rotten with treason.

Treachery is hard to avoid or define during rebellion, but James' supporters later antedated the facts, and argued that he was led, by vile craft, to his ruin. Sunderland's career might, indeed, give colour to this theory. He was pocketing a French pension, while his wife, through Sidney, impressed her husband's merits upon Orange; in summer he attended the Mass, in December he was a refugee in Holland, by 1690 he was openly in William's favour. But ambition to be safe at any price, personal extravagance, and gambling debts seem to explain this base politician's game, and he may be cleared of intellectual perfidy at the cost of his heart. For he had quarrelled with Petre's section, advised against prosecuting the bishops, and (like Godolphin and Dartmouth) advised a speedy meeting of Parliament.

It was on the advice of this moderate party that James tacked about on his course. He cancelled the Ecclesiastical Commission, restored the Magdalen Fellows, and gave back

a few town charters. But he still refused to
meet Parliament, and all his steps were halting
and insincere. Having alternately persecuted
and petted Dissenters, he now tried to wheedle
back the Anglicans, and attempted to separate
the spiritual from the lay peers. In late
October, overjoyed by reports of disaster to
William's fleet, he dismissed Sunderland.

If a clear, candid course were needed at home,
it was far more urgent abroad. In June the
Elector of Cologne died. In August the French
prepared to invade Germany. The same
month Innocent XI pronounced against
Furstenburg. In late September French
troops seized Papal Avignon, and besieged
the imperial city of Philipsburg. The stars
in their courses fought for Orange, since these
aggressions spared Holland the onslaught,
freed his hands to invade England, and brought
Catholic Europe to his side. Yet James
helped the stars. Louis sent him warning
after warning, offered him a French squadron,
even hesitated whether, in England's interests,
it were not better to attack Holland before
Germany. James refused the ships, and
declined to provoke Holland into war. Both
sides asked for decision. The States-General
intimated that conciliation in England was the
prelude to peace in Europe : Louis, naturally

suspicious, left him (save for a little money) to fall alone.

We need not follow the stages in his doom. At the second attempt William sailed successfully, and on the 5th November landed, with 24,000 troops, in Torbay. Even now the King would neither negotiate nor summon Parliament. In Wiltshire, in his own presence, his army turned traitor. Simultaneously, risings broke out in North and Midlands, and Anne joined the rebels; the chief ports and arsenals, Portsmouth, Hull, and Newcastle, were surrendered or betrayed. All England clamoured for a free Protestant Parliament. The rising generation were allied with veterans; Dick Steele was riding in a troop of horse, Robert Harley was up in the West. But anti-foreign feeling was strong, and a resolute stand might have won fair compromise. James, who had been firm over-long, now suddenly collapsed. He named commissioners to negotiate, but meant throughout to fly; he feared his father's fate. Having sent the Queen and her infant to France some days earlier, on the 11th December, at three in the morning, he stole out of Whitehall and made for the Thames.

He had disposed of the great seal, burned the writs for Parliament, ordered Dartmouth

to take his loyal ships to Tyrconnel, and bade
Feversham disband the army. He would
neither defend his throne nor contribute to
settlement. This was the end. Held up at
Faversham, and brought back to London, he
never intended to stay, nor did William mean
to let him. The mass of English politicians
did not mean it either. The Whigs had joined
the invasion *en masse*, and were talking of a
cession of the throne. The Tory Danby, now
almost viceroy of the North, refused to accept
James' messages; Halifax went over to the
winning side. A strong London party pressed
for drastic settlement. Even High-church-
men asked a free Parliament, and were ready
to give Orange wide provisional powers. The
King's first flight reduced London to two days
of anarchy; in a real sense, he had " abdi-
cated," and the settlement, whatever shape
it might take, was thereby removed from his
hands. The Dutch guards were already in
St. James'.

" Frighted away," or of his free will, on the
23rd December James left Rochester, the last
refuge he had himself selected, and on
Christmas day landed in France, whither his
Queen and Louis XIV had long beckoned him.
Save from the deck of a French transport bound
for Ireland, he was not to see England again.

CHAPTER XII

THE INTELLECTUAL BACKGROUND

THE human mind, which creates forms and institutions, is the last thing to be tamed by its creatures, and cannot be docketed in centuries. If no fixed date can be given for the " origin " of Renaissance, Cabinet, or domestic system of industry, more impossible is it to say, " Here ends the medieval, there begins the modern mind." The stuff of history is old, though re-dyed in new colours and shot with new schemes, and any English lives show the continuity of intellectual influence. Burghley, who was born in 1520, and must often have seen his grandfather, Henry VII's servant, was still minister when Ben Jonson wrote his first comedy; Jonson lived to know the Puritan lawyer Maynard who, as doyen of the Bar, welcomed William of Orange. If the Renaissance was the dawn of modern England, the full sun was long in rising, and its setting cannot be put earlier than Milton's death in 1674. Yet, a time does come, marked rather by change of temperature than by gradations of darkness and light, when we feel the mass of Englishmen to be more like ourselves than like contemporaries of Colet and More.

What causes brought that change about have been suggested above—the classical revival, theological revolution, maritime discovery, change in money values, a new vision of the State. Whichever of these be taken as cause or effect, it is at least clear that the whole story was conditioned by immense increase of wealth and by the spread of printing; of these two, one certain consequence was increased education, which in its turn conditioned all else. It is possible that in pure learning medieval English doctors surpassed their posterity—that clerical and feminine education were better in the fifteenth than in the seventeenth century. But it is certain that education in the latter period was more widely ramified among the laity, and that learning was more closely linked than before, or since, to public affairs. The Tudors and James I were most learned of British sovereigns. Their teachers, Cheke, Ascham, or Buchanan, were eminent humanists. The proportion of scholars in high office can be judged from the lives of More, Bacon, and

Wotton, or later from Selden, Falkland, and
Clarendon, Lauderdale, Temple, and Burnet.
Anglicanism, which began with Cranmer
and Jewel, produced prodigies of learning in
Hooker, Usher, Jeremy Taylor, Pearson and
Bull. The ratio of University graduates to
population was probably larger than to-day;
they were certainly drawn from a wider circle
of schools. Royal interest in the Universities,
abused to promote place-hunters or to censor
literature, was seen at its best in new foundations and chairs. If the Reformation despoiled many old endowments, the century
was prolific in new, such as those given to
St. Paul's, Shrewsbury, Rugby, and Westminster schools; Busby at Westminster, as
Mulcaster at the Merchant Taylor's, illustrate
the hold of great schoolmasters over several
generations. The printing-press, a luxury
for humanists and nobles in Henry VII's day,
was a familiar weapon of controversy to
Walsingham and Peter Wentworth, and from
the Civil War onwards became, in cheap
pamphlets and newspapers, the creator of
common opinion.

Yet the Middle Ages died hard, and a curious
lull separates the " Utopia " and the " New
Atlantis." It is true that a hair shirt is not
incompatible with mental speculation; that

More's " Utopia," under the guise of a Platonic commonwealth, criticized the age for its lack of tolerance, its indiscriminate punishment, its warlike royalty. Yet More himself was medieval, and the *Civitas Dei* the background of his ideal; his friend Colet, interpreter of St. Paul, was not the last Dean of St. Paul's to be in advance of his age. Taken as a whole, literature in the first half of the century had scarcely advanced in motive upon that of the Yorkists. Apart from the foreigners who wrote lives of Henry VII, history was still of the chronicle type represented by Wriothesley, and no ardent Protestanism could lend critical gifts to Edward Hall, Henry VIII's London partizan. The study of institutions was virtually limited to legal abstracts, editions of the statutes, or treatises on the justice of the peace. Skelton, the satirist of Wolsey, or Elyot's " Governor," the mystery plays of Coventry, Latimer's sermons, all speak the language of the previous century, a native and naive English thought, with barely a veneer of Renaissance.

It is only in Henry VIII's last years, in the period of gloom that began about 1540 and stretched to 1570, that, with Ascham's appearance in prose and Surrey's in verse, the Renaissance seems to descend from the skies to

English streets, and move into its formative
age. The humanism earlier borrowed from
Italy, and taught in English Universities by
the Dutch Erasmus or the Spaniard Vives,
was transmitted now through Englishmen,
but the direct influence of the classics and
Continental letters was still overwhelming.
Elizabethan translations perpetuated the
great names of all nations in resplendent
prose; North's "Plutarch" and Chapman's
"Homer" have won most from immortality,
but Tasso, Machiavelli, Commines, Montaigne,
or Calvin, became as familiar as the ancient
world. The perfected sonnet of Sidney or
Shakespeare sums up hundreds of experiments on French and Italian models; Ron-
sard and the Pleiade impressed the French
lily on the English lyric; Spain was stamped
on English drama. Lyly's Euphuism owed
much to Castiglione; the Platonic ideal inspired Spenser; the cold morals and the warm
imagery of Italy are seen in the aguish
tragedy of Marlowe. Between 1580 and 1620
intellectual Europe was deeply cosmopolitan;
giants of erudition on either side, Bellarmine
or Baronius for the Catholics, Scaliger or the
Casaubons for Protestants, contested the
world's future, in an arena thronged by all
the learned of Europe.

In England, as elsewhere, the secondary but most lasting effect of the Renaissance was that pride of country and native tongue, which all nations in renaissance experience. It ranged from the reasoned decision of scholars like Ascham to write in English, to the ballad cycles of Robin Hood, the rude plays built round persons so dubious as King Arthur or Jane Shore, or the patriotic drama produced by the Armada. Chroniclers like Holingshed, who gave Shakespeare his raw material, were followed by a long line of antiquaries in Bale, Lambarde, or Leland, by citizens of no mean city, of whom John Stow is the abiding type; finally by the finished work of Camden, of Bacon's " Henry VII " or Knolles' " History of the Turks," which superseded chronicle by a critical, comparative, narrative. Accompanying this conscious patriotism was that Renaissance quality instilled by all humanists from the Italians to Sidney or Hakluyt, the wedding of letters to action. Sidney's death in battle at Zutphen could be matched by Donne's experience at Cadiz, or Lodge's in the Straits of Magellan; his teaching echoes Elyot and Ascham, who bade Englishmen learn Greek and stick to the bow. The diverse learning dedicated to Elizabeth or Essex was meant to have a real application; the art of living, or of ruling

men, was not held to be different in kind from
that of the epic.   In this sense all Renaissance
art was didactic, and Raleigh and Milton alike
men of action.

Causes for the sudden upspringing of literature in a nation appear to defy prosaic analysis.
But the century's new discoveries, of letters
and creeds, of men and continents, fell in England on a people exceptional in national unity,
deeply aristocratic, predominantly rural, more
tuneful than æsthetic.   Of these conditions
the twin harvest was lyric and drama, an
unequalled development, in one people at one
time, of intellect and passion.   For one generation the soil, fertilized by peace, wealth, knowledge, and achievement, seemed to blossom
as without labour ; innumerable anthologies of
songs, pages of detached beauty in the worst
dramatists, show a fertility of excellence more
explicable by nature than by art.

Fifteenth-century art and music in England
had gone hand in hand with an admirable lyric
gift, found in all districts, in cities and monasteries, and the flood of poetry after 1580 is not
so new in inspiration as in volume, subtlety,
and mastery of form.   Elizabethan lyric had
more continuous connection than the drama
with old England, and it sprang in profusion
from every corner of society.   Shakespeare's

songs do not surpass in art the best work of a
score of others—of Lodge, Fletcher, Campion,
Carew, or the anonymous authors of the song-
books; all alike have the same fancy of heart
and head, the veracity to nature which we
associate with the clear-cut distance of early
morning.

The body of Elizabethan drama, which may
be said to begin in 1590 with Marlowe and to
end with Massinger at the Civil war, is itself
enough to mark that the Middle Ages have
gone. Both chronicle play and ballads,
Henry V and Agincourt, keep a connection of
subject with older days, but the spirit they
contain is new. The moralities which the
Church had taught, or allowed to be drama-
tized, are departed; their knell is rung by
Marlowe's " thirst for unrighteousness." Man,
like Faustus, makes his own hell. Warfare
from rediscovered ancient worlds, " to ride in
triumph through Persepolis," a longing for
strange new seas, the Bermoothes and all the
elements conquerable by man, all this trans-
ported the narrow stage of the Rose or the
Globe. This unmoral energy, which over-
turns worlds in Marlowe, descended to Ford
and Webster, and makes wearisome the
Spanish tragedies, the woes of Hecuba, the
lust and incest, which fed with strong meat the

groundlings jaded by lions at the Tower. Only Shakespeare's mature work provided a divine comedy of human life, built on foundations which would outlast any one generation. The problems round " Lear," " Hamlet," or " Othello," the moral issues raised in the " Tempest " or " Measure for Measure," have pierced the theological horizons of the Middle Ages. His stage is the whole universe of thought rediscovered by the Renaissance; his drama, like the Arminian movement or the new political theory, deduced the scheme of life from human character and its freedom of will, and made man, Bacon's " servant and interpreter of nature," the often unhappy but not inglorious agent of a Divine plan.

Representing, as in Greece, the rule of a capital over a commonwealth of artizans and peasants, the drama is the best expression of the many elements that made Elizabeth's kingdom. Its special patrons were the Court and the nobles, and at high festivals, till the Civil War, the Court's amusement continued to be the masque, on which Henry VIII spent so much money and capering. A fantastic blend of legend and chivalry, abstract charities and virtues, and the Arcadian woodlands which furnished the loves and sports of kings, engaged the talent of Jonson and his tribe, of

Inigo Jones and Henry Lawes; Leicester, Buckhurst, Southampton, and other magnates, financed dramatic companies. Protests from Puritan aldermen were crushed by powerful patrons and popular demand; the players' trumpets drowned the bells calling the godly to prayer. Considerable fortunes left by actor-managers, by Alleyn, founder of Dulwich College, or Shakespeare himself, testify to the numbers who made the play their chief recreation. Touring companies were welcomed not only by small English towns but in foreign courts, at Elsinore or on the coast of Bohemia. Not only classical or British mythology, but contemporary politics, became material for the drama. Essex challenged the Queen with a performance of *Richard II*; the Puritans and the Pilgrim Fathers were brought on the stage, before the deluge. An active university drama linked classical education to modern life, and protracted every royal visit. The scope of dramatic talent could be illustrated in the lyric gift and grace of Beaumont and Fletcher, by the tragic power of Ford, the popular comedies of Dekker, Heywood, or Marston; it lasted till the Civil War and beyond it, with Cartwright and Shirley. Shakespeare's effortless superiority as poet and craftsman crowns the romantic drama,

and summarizes like none since Dante all the
hopes and aspirations of an age. The tre-
mendous forces of death and nature that beset
Lear, or make Caliban, no more exhaust this
universal mind than plain men's conversations
in Warwickshire and Cotswolds, or that
analysis of love and company with which his
women make delightful the Renaissance.
Familiar quotation and ceaseless production
of his plays in his lifetime, the applause of
Kings, fellow-artists, and City audiences—
this at least must vindicate the taste of the
Elizabethans.

With his death in 1616, the mirror he held
up to nature, the equilibrium and *élan* of that
sane generation, may be said to have broken.
Jonson and Donne, the two greatest survivors,
would suggest it. Both were bred Catholics;
both reacted against the spontaneous, satisfied
Protestant England of their youth. Bacon's
rather facile optimism failed to content the
coming age. Jonson stigmatized the monstrous extravagance, the flabby humours that
marked a romantic movement in decline, and
returning to classical forms breathed much of
the classic contempt for the crimes and follies
that make up the history of man. Donne's
satires spiritualized the feuds, harpies, and
utopias which Dekker and others painted in

gross colours from the new growing London.
In Donne intellect and passion are no longer
in agreement, but at war. Like Falkland,
he travelled far to find truth, and found her
only in the cragged hills; there he wrestled
and would not let her go, until she blessed
him. The "metaphysical" school of whom
he was the chief turned in upon themselves,
or their destiny, the Elizabethans' dissecting
power, and poetry became a spiritual anatomy.

A wind of many doctrines released by the
Reformation was, in short, buffeting the mind
of the early seventeenth century. Protestant
individualism was haunted by Catholic revival,
classical morality jostled with mysticism and
new science. In some, like Carew, Suckling,
or Herrick, a Latin paganism triumphed;
the singing gift went on, but honour became
illusion, ideals a weariness, and a carven skull
sits beside the laughing loves. Falkland and
Sir Thomas Browne, absorbing all knowledge,
fell back on dreams or the Catholic faith of
intellectual second childhood—*credo ut intelli-
gam.* Catholic teaching, Spanish models,
disgust with a Calvinism almost non-thinking,
drove a host of fine minds to poetic Laudianism, and the "divine" school of Herbert,
Vaughan, and Crashaw lent fervour to the
cause for which the Gorings or the Wilmots

Q

drew their fleshly sword. A common sense
of disillusion, a wish to rest in something
ancient and assured, whether Catholic or
natural, a distrust of Bible theology and mob-
law—all this cast a not ignoble shadow over
English letters under the second Stuart.

On the other half of this revolving orb
the planets of Renaissance and Reformation
blazed for a last time brightly in Milton, in
whom (as in lesser men like Hutchinson or
Marvell) learning, Puritanism, and passionate
love of freedom still created the universals
of the true Elizabethan. It is true that
an acrid period of twenty years' pamphlet-
eering separated the first grace of " Comus "
and " Lycidas " from " Paradise Lost " and
" Samson Agonistes,"—twenty years, in
which all that Milton lived for triumphed,
only to perish. Yet " Paradise Lost " has
that universal scheme, that reduction of all
things to one, that amalgam of religion and
knowledge, which is Elizabethan, if not
medieval, and disappears with the compartments that, in modern life, wall poetry off
from the everyday life of society. The last
of the Puritans was also the last English
humanist; Renaissance and Reformation died,
as they were born, together.

Not unfittingly, in this age of growing

precision, English prose attained its final form. Shedding the imported pedantries of Euphuism, it long kept the music, colour, and " shoots of everlastingness " that livened Elizabethan verse, and in the Authorised Version, in Burton's " Anatomy," in Donne's sermons, or in Browne, displayed the depth of English speech. In the prose of the middle period, Jeremy Taylor or Clarendon, lingers some of this grandeur of earlier days, but Fuller's conceits, or Walton's pathos, strike us as archaic, and the admirable candour and clarity of Cowley more truly anticipates the Restoration.

French supremacy in European culture, the perfection of its lissom and effective language, the triumph of reason over divinity and passion, a conscious imitation of classic forms, all this produced the prose and poetry of Waller and Denham, Dryden, Sprat, Temple, and Halifax— to make that instrument which Addison, Swift, and Pope employed to curb both dullness and originality. Increasing differentiation of classes inevitably assisted separation in taste and humour; Shakespeare's or Dekker's wit was written down as unbefitting the gentry; the " Tempest " was remodelled by Davenant, the " Canterbury Tales " by Dryden, to please a more classic taste and sophisticated gentility.

True, a heroic drama made various fortunes
for Nell Gwyn or Dryden, but this was not the
characteristic product of an age of common
sense. New social conditions, rationalism,
and literary convention, tended rather to
polished lyric verse, political satire, essay,
and the comedy of manners; in all but the
last Dryden was supreme—a literary dictator
like none till Samuel Johnson. His opportunist temper fitted that generation like a
glove; with masculine fearlessness he demonstrated that the language, like the Sabbath, was made for man, and not the converse;
that plain diction had its own strength. A
dozen others—Rochester, Roscommon, Sedley,
or Dorset—turned out good examples of the
cool lyric which Waller had made the fashion.
Dryden's epistles were matched by the trans-
parent and winning prose in which Sprat wrote
the story of the Royal Society, or Halifax "The
Trimmer." Incidental literature, like pamphlets of L'Estrange and Marvell, Shaftesbury's
fragment of autobiography, the rich plainness
of Bunyan or Burnet, show the gain in
directness and argumentation since the days of
Bacon, or those of the early Hobbes.

Political satire, familiar in ballad and
broadsheet, was highly developed by a generation bred upon Horace, Juvenal, and Lucian,

and desirous to turn by rapid strokes the opinion of a small but interested audience. The rude vigour of Civil War satirists like Cleveland was polished in Butler's " Hudibras," or Marvell's scathing verses against the Court; in "Absalom and Achitophel," " the Medal," and " The Hind and the Panther," Dryden carried the art as far as English can go.

The historical writing of this century (often published much later), whether full-dress narrative, memoir, or collections, showed a great advance upon Bacon's standards. Herbert of Cherbury's " Henry VIII," Clarendon's " Rebellion," or Burnet in his " Reformation " and " History of My Own Time," manifest a consciousness that even pronounced views need support from documents and real material. This was provided for them by men like Rushworth, by owners of libraries like Cotton, booksellers like Thomason, or chroniclers like Phillips. Personal papers, as the diaries of Pepys or Reresby, Roger North's lives of his brothers, or Temple's memoirs, are examples only of a great mass, showing a sympathy with character, wide intellectual interest, and a sense of the complexity of government, which were common to many English men of affairs. The papers

of Lady Russell, of Dorothy Osborne, Mary
Rich, or Mrs. Hutchinson, prove that educated
women had not all died with Elizabeth;
the libraries and correspondence of innumerable
county families, that it is unsafe to generalize
from London playwrights as to the barbarous
illiteracy of the squires.

No change was greater or more rapid than
in the method and conception of philosophy
and natural science. In spite of Tudor
creations like the college of Physicians, of
pioneers like William Gilbert and virtuosos
like Bacon, astrology and witchcraft troubled
the Stuart theologians and judges, and it was
not till the middle of the century that an
advance in force began. Then Thomas Hobbes
published the speculations he had discussed
with Descartes and Gassendi; Wren, Ward,
and Petty founded the Royal Society; Harvey
and Sydenham began a long line of famous
doctors. After the Restoration the names of
Boyle, Isaac Newton, Halley, Flamstead, Ray,
or Cumberland, even the presence on the
bishops' bench of Wilkins and Seth Ward,
may testify to the wealth of this new learning,
and to the fresh standpoint from which the
structure and dynamics of life were judged.

This revolution, so clear in letters and
science, transformed also men's thinking about

the State. There are, it is true, a line of typically English writers, from the Lancastrian Fortescue to Elizabeth's secretary, Thomas Smith, or the royalist Clarendon, who, perhaps, best represent average opinion, for the very reason that they professed facts more than principles, and historical rather than rational grounds for political obedience. Such men agreed upon the Crown's supremacy in the State, and its divinely-ordered rule, but declared it limited by law—whether by God's law that binds a good ruler, or by natural reason, or by the common law and statute, embodying the King's voluntary concessions. The rôle of this moderate but pragmatic school in politics was useful, yet indecisive, for it has been seen that sixteenth-century conditions asked, and evoked, more clear-cut ideas of sovereignty. Ultimately from its religious and political warfare two rival principles emerged—the divinity of the King, and the sovereignty of the people. Each had its cross-currents and qualifications; for the first could be watered down to the sanctity of order, the second construed as the rule of aristocracy. The law and theology dominating that age were susceptible of many interpretations; an appeal to nature might end either in acceptance of kingship as the survival of the

fittest, or in the natural equality of all men.
But whatever the rendering of the faith,
under these two heads can be brought all the
political theory of the century and a half that
followed Luther. Of the two, the liberal
conclusion that the sovereign is limited,
flowed more naturally from medieval pre-
cept and practice. The habitual teaching of
Catholicism, that the State is subordinate to
the higher law which the Church interprets,
was eagerly taken up alike by Jesuit and
Presbyterian, while Selden and Halifax could
have discovered warrant for their notion of
limited monarchy in Bracton, or the " Song
of Lewes." In this camp, too, must be
reckoned the illustrious Hooker, who assumed
that the State rested on a contract, incorporat-
ing " the grand mandates of morality." But
the most significant exponents of this new
literature reached a medieval conclusion by a
modern route, postulating not so much the
majesty of God seen in the law of His Church,
as the majesty of the equal rights of man.
From this intense individualism sprang the
Commonwealth Levellers' demand for the
power of the community; its root was disclosed as the century wore out in the individualist mediocrity of John Locke.

Practical politics create English political

thought, and the radicalism of the Commonwealth men from Edward VI's time onwards
impelled the State Church to formulate its
defensive theory of the divine right of kings.
Compared with this, the influence of the
Roman law and the civilians, of Machiavelli
or the Italians familiar to Thomas Cromwell
and Bacon, was as slight as that of Aristotle's
regimental view of society. The Church's
homilies, making rebellion the sin of witchcraft, had primarily in mind those who, in
God's name, challenged the existing order.
On the Continent the penalty of anarchy had
received such fearful illustration that this
theory of passive obedience played for a
season a valid part in history, and Scriptural
renderings of liberty were so conflicting, that
it was as well that St. Paul had taught undeviating obedience to the powers that be.
The Apostle's lesson was pushed by Hobbes,
the acutest thinker of the age, to lengths
undreamed of by Anglicans, and placed on a
basis that would justify the rule of a heretic
or usurper. Yet, omitting his derisory use of
the contract forming the State, and his view
of a mechanical selfish fearfulness as the
motive of society, Hobbes stressed, as none
had before, the two points which Strafford
and the Commons had arrived at in practical

politics—power as the sanction of law, and the necessary unity of ruler and ruled. His unorthodox foundations scandalized a devout age, and his immediate successors, the Cavalier Filmer or the republican Sidney, made little advance on the old rivals of passive obedience and the original contract. The shock of Charles I's execution and the war gave new life to the first; the Whigs, infuriated by James II, repeated the other, which in the Bill of Rights became the official theory of 1688.

But Hobbes himself mellowed despotic teaching by making room for utility as the test of institutions, and admitted that obedience could be withdrawn from a sovereign beaten in the field. Divine right, too, as read in that century, had its limitations; Anglicans were pledged to obey rather the *de facto* ruler than legitimism, while Filmer made Nature, not Scripture, the ground of paternal authority. These were the first straws blown on a mighty wind, unsettling the fixed altars of earlier theory. The sanction of institutions was henceforth rather their existence than their righteousness, their conformity to nature more than their descent from heaven, their result and working instead of their origin. The " fundamental " laws of God and man were to be rewritten in the terms of changing human experience.

The two centuries, which had undergone such change and passion, ended on this note of moderation; in Dryden, Tillotson, and Locke, experimental philosophy, and the newspaper, and after Latimer, Drake, or Strafford it may seem a bathos. Yet a country pays, after all, for unrestrained ideals, and a Bank of England makes a better terminus than a Bastille. In the hundred years that began with Elizabeth most of the solid achievements of our race received their impetus; three-quarters of the seventeenth century were spent in impressing on Elizabethan vitality the forms and conventions which must perpetuate both *imperium et libertas.* In the building of their manor-houses, as in the structure of their government or their prose, we may see, not unreasonably, that rhythm resting in restraint, which marks in this strong generation a rare balance of man and master, emotion and intelligence, nature and art.

BIBLIOGRAPHY

(The original note has been amended in some particulars for
the reprint of 1942; some works published since 1927
are now included.)

FIVE great historians have covered most of the period:
Clarendon, "History of the Rebellion" (specially Vol. I)
is much of it genuinely contemporary; *Froude,* "History
of England" (at its best in dealing with Elizabeth),
and some of the "Short Studies"; *Ranke,* "History of
England," which begins in detail at 1625 and is specially
valuable for foreign affairs; *Gardiner,* "History of England,
1603–42," "Great Civil War," and "Commonwealth and
Protectorate"; *Macaulay,* "History of England," for the
Revolution.

The modern scholarship, which corrects and supplements
these pioneers, may be illustrated as follows:—

A. For the Tudor Period. *Busch,* "Henry VII"; *Pollard,*
"Political History of England, 1547–1603," and his bio-
graphies of Henry VIII and Wolsey; *Pickthorn,* "Early
Tudor Government"; *Chambers,* "Thomas More"; *Merri-
man,* "Thomas Cromwell"; *Dixon,* "History of the Church
of England" and *Frere's* volume (1558–1603) in *Stephens and
Hunt,* "History of the Church of England"; *J. E. Neale,*
"Queen Elizabeth"; *Read,* "Walsingham," and *J. A.
Williamson,* "The Age of Drake," for aspects of Elizabethan
foreign policy; *Cheyney,* "History of England from the Defeat
of the Armada," and *Notestein,* "Winning of the Initiative by
the House of Commons," are specially useful for parliamentary
development and institutions.

B. The Stuarts. Two volumes of the Oxford History,
G. Davies, "The Early Stuarts," and *G. N. Clark,* "The Later
Stuarts"; and *G. M. Trevelyan,* "England Under the Stuarts,"
for the whole century. For the Protectorate period, many
works and articles of *Sir Charles Firth*; notably "Cromwell,"
"Cromwell's Army," and "The Last Two Years of the Protectorate." Charles II's reign may perhaps best be read by
combining *Airy's* edition of *Burnet,* "History of My Own
Time," with *Ogg,* "The Reign of Charles II." *Masson,*

"Life and Times of Milton," *Feiling,* "The Tory Party, 1640–1714," and *Foxcroft,* "Halifax," illustrate the origins of party; *Braithwaite,* "The Beginnings of Quakerism," *Trevor-Roper,* "Laud," *Shaw,* "The Church under the Commonwealth," and *Bate,* "The Declaration of Indulgence," for different angles of the religious problem.

C. Constitutional History. *Tanner,* "Tudor Constitutional Documents," *Gardiner,* "Constitutional Documents of the Puritan Revolution," and *Grant Robertson,* "Select Statutes, Cases, and Documents," give a body of important texts, with introductions and notes; *Hallam,* "Constitutional History," the view of a Whig of 1832, is always suggestive: a more modern outlook and new light on special problems, may be found in *McIlwain,* "The High Court of Parliament," *Reid,* "The King's Council in the North," and *Evans,* "The Principal Secretary of State." For general reference see *Keir,* "Constitutional History of Modern Britain," and *W. S. Holdsworth,* "History of English Law," which shows the struggle between Common Law and its rivals.

D. Among other works deserving mention in regard to particular aspects. *Maynard Smith,* "Pre-Reformation England"; *Cunningham,* "Growth of English Industry and Commerce"; *Lipson,* "Economic History of England," Vols. II and III; *W. R. Scott,* "History of Joint-Stock Companies," Vol. I; *Tawney,* "The Agrarian Problem in the 16th Century"; *Hume Brown,* "History of Scotland," Vol. II; *Hooker,* "Ecclesiastical Polity," Book V (ed. Church and Paget); *Corbett,* "Drake and the Tudor Navy"; *Williamson,* "British Expansion," a short exposition of a subject more fully dealt with by *Osgood,* "The American Colonies in the 17th Century"; *Lecky,* "History of Ireland," has a *résumé* of the whole period, while more detail is in *Bagwell,* "Ireland under the Tudors," sections of *Gardiner's* works, and *Burghclere,* "Ormonde." The *Cambridge History of English Literature* may be consulted for full account of originals and modern books. Of modern works upon the political ideas of the age, reference may be made to *Figgis,* "The Divine Right of Kings," and *Gooch,* "English Democratic Ideas in the Seventeenth Century."

INDEX

(This index contains only selected details. Main subjects and persons will be found by means of the chapter headings.)

AMERICA, 8, 40, 103–4, 174, 203
Anne, Princess, 209, 222, 228
Argyle, eighth Earl, 207; ninth Earl, 212
Arlington, 192–4, 200
Arminians, 125
Articles, the Six, 60; the Thirty-nine, 123
Ascham, 231, 235

Bacon, Francis, 133–4, 240, 246
Battles :
Stoke, 21; Flodden, 35; Pavia, 37; Pinkie, 72; Edgehill, 155; Marston Moor, 155; Naseby, 156; Philiphaugh, 156; Preston, 160; Dunbar, 164; Worcester, 164; the Dunes, 179; Sedgemoor, 213
Baxter, 212
Bible, 40–1, 57, 61, 243
Bishops, the Seven, 224–6
Boleyn, family of, 44, 52, 90
Buckingham, first Villiers Duke of, 135, 138–40; second duke, 192
Bunyan, 244
Burnet, 221, 244

Cabal, 192–4
Calais, 8, 27, 78, 83
Catharine of Aragon, 31, 33–5, 44–5, 52, 59
Catharine of Braganza, 198, 204
Churchill, John, 202, 223, 226
Clarendon, first Hyde Earl of, 146, 148, 182, 186, 188–92
Cloth trade, 27, 106, 131, 174
Coke, Sir Edward, 112, 116, 133
Colonies, 106, 154, 174, 178, 203
Common Law, 111–13, 116, 134

Companies, chartered, 105, 174, 202
Constitutional problems :
Council, 23–5, 38, 111, 115; of the North, 24, 116, 135; Star Chamber, 24, 38, 108, 146; of the Marches, 62; privilege of Parliament, 64, 117, 132; martial law, 116, 134; Petition of Right, 134; Grand Remonstrance, 147; Heads of the Proposals, 159; Humble Petition and Advice, 169; Instrument of Government, 168, 171
Cranmer, Archbishop, 50, 70, 74, 79
Cromwell, Thomas, 50, 54, 60
Currency, 63, 67, 85

Danby, 185–6, 194–6, 201, 212, 223, 225, 229
Darnley, 92–3
De La Pole, family of, 21
Devereux, Robert, second Earl of Essex, 90, 99–100, 109
Donne, 240, 243
Drama, 237 ff.
Dryden, 243–5
Dudley, John Duke of Northumberland and Earl of Warwick, 67, 72–5
Dudley, Robert Earl of Leicester, 88, 90, 98–9
Dunkirk, 179, 198

Eliot, Sir John, 130, 153
Elizabeth, Queen of Bohemia, 139
Enclosures, 11, 28, 71, 107, 205
Euphuism, 234, 243

Fairfax, 156–7, 160, 162, 172
Falkland, 146
Filmer, 250

254

Fisher, Bishop, 49, 53
Francis I, 35, 37, 59
Frobisher, 99, 103
Furstenburg, 219, 227

Gardiner, Bishop, 70, 76, **78**
Gondomar, 139
Gresham, 85
Grey, family of, 75, 92
Guilds, 29, 68, 106
Guises, 83–4, 96

Hale, Matthew, 172, 176
Halifax, George Savile, Marquess of, 197, 209, 212, 214, 223, 243
Hampden, 145, 156
Henrietta Maria, 140–1, 148–9
Herbert, George, 241
Heresy laws, 69, 76.
High Commission, 111, 116–17, 123–4, 133, 143, 146
Historical literature, 233, 235, 245
Hobbes, 244, 246, 249–50
Hooker, 125, 248

Independents, 121, 154, 157 ff.
India, 103, 105–6, 174, 204
Industry, regulation of, 28, 106–7, 131, 205
Ireland:
    Tudor government of, 62, 97, 100; plantations, 101–2, 142; Strafford, 135, 141; Cromwellian conquest, 163, 175; Ormonde, 163, 206; Tyrconnel, 215–17, 223, 229
Ireton, 158–9, 161, 175

Jamaica, 179
Jeffreys, Judge, 209, 213–14
Jonson, 230, 240
Justices of the peace, 25, 106–7, 113, 205

Knox, John, 74, 83, **144**

Lambert, General, 160, 172, 180–1
Latimer, 60, 68, 79
Laud, 125, 136, 149
Lauderdale, 183, 195, 207
Levellers, 129, 172–3
London, 28, 46, 75, 152
Louis XIV, 193, 198, 201, 219–21, 227
Ludlow, Edmund, 172, 175
Lyric poetry, 234, 236, 244

Magdalen College, 217, 226

Maritime discovery, 40, 103–5
Marlowe, 234, 237
Martyrs: under Mary, 79; under Elizabeth, 94
Maximilian I, Emperor, 35
Mercantilism, 27, 106, 202
Milton, 153, 176, 242
Monasticism, 47, 54–7
Monk, 172, 175, 181–3
Monmouth, James Duke of, 196–7, 213
Montague, Edward Lord Sandwich, 179, 184
Montrose, 155–6, 163
More, Sir Thomas, 15, 39, 42, 49, **53**

Navy, 27, 105, 152, 179–80, 199
New Model Army, 151, 156
New York, 199
Norfolk, second Howard Duke of, 22, 24, 44; third duke, 49, 62, 64; fourth duke, 90, 93

Orange, Princes of, 97, 99, **177**, 199 201, 219–29

Paget, 73, 76, 85
Parker, Archbishop, 89
Parliament:
    Development of, 37, 64, 114, **129**; "packing" of, 48, 64, 76; Long Parliament, 145, 158, 164–7; Barebones', 167; Cavalier, 190 ff.
Pepys, 179, 245
Plots and Rebellions:
    Simnel, 21; Warbeck, 21, 28; Cornish, 22, 70; Pilgrimage of Grace, 58; Ket, 71; Northern earls, 93; Babington, 98; Gunpowder, 118; Army, 145; Popish, 195–6
Pole, family of, 22, 59, 78
Political theory, 114, 154, 247 ff.
Popes:
    Julius II, 44; Clement VII, 44, 52; Paul III, 59; Pius V, 93, 118; Innocent XI, 215–16, 227
Prayer-books, 57, 70, 74, 81
Presbyterians, 120–1, 157, 172
Press, development of the, 10, 115, 176, 232
Prose, changes in English, **233**, 243 ff.
Puritanism, 73, 91, 120, 151, **153**
Pym, 130, 134, 145, 155

Raleigh, 103, 106–7, **139**

Regicides, 162, 189

Revenues, figures of, 17, 25, 174, 189, 202

Rochester, Laurence Hyde, Earl of, 197, 212, 217

Royal Society, 176, 244, 246

Russell, family of, 67, 72, 210

Satire, political, 244–5

Scotland :
Early Tudor relations with, 32, 63; Elizabethan policy towards, 83, 93, 99; efforts at Union, 129, 168; in the Civil Wars, 143 ff., 155, 159; under Cromwell, 175; under Lauderdale, 207

Selden, 117, 151

Seymour, Edward Lord Hertford and Earl of Somerset, 63, 66–72

Shaftesbury, first Earl of, 151, 182, 192, 194–7

Shakespeare, 238–40

Sidney, Philip, 234–5

Smith, Sir Thomas, 66, 91, 247

Spain, alliance with, 31–7, 59, 77, 83, 94 ff., 138–40

Speakers of the Commons, 39, 64, 115

Spenser, 100–1, 234

Statutes :
Of fines, 23; *de facto* title, 23; Star Chamber, 24; Navigation, 27; Poor Laws, 29, 68, 107, 205; Supremacy, 51, 81, 123; appeals, 52; Monasteries, 55–6, 58, 76; proclamations, 64, 69; Uniformity, 70, 74, 82, 123, 190; Labourers, 106; Tri-

ennial parliaments, 146; Ireland, 175, 206; Habeas Corpus, 186, 214; "Clarendon" code, 188–90; Test Act, 194, 214 ff.

Strafford, Thomas Wentworth Earl of, 135, 141, 146

Sunderland, second Earl of, 197, 209, 212, 215, 226–7

Tangier, 204

Taxation, unconstitutional, 25, 38, 63, 116, 131–2

Temple, Sir William, 200, 245

Theologians, schools of, 71, 125, 136, 157, 176

Thirty Years' War, 139

Thurloe, 173, 176

Toleration, 54, 121, 157–9, 177, 188

Tories, 194, 197, 209, 212, 214, 218

Treaties :
Magnus Intercursus, 28; Etaples, 31; Medina del Campo, 31; Cambrai, 45; Edinburgh, 84; Breda, 199; Dover, 193; Westminster, 194; Nimwegen, 219

Triple Alliance, 200

Ulster, 101–2, 142, 206

Universities, 40, 45, 71, 150, 176, 217, 232

Vane, Sir Henry, 160, 172, 179, 189

Walsingham, 90, 96, 99

Whigs, 194–7, 209, 217, 225

Whitgift, 121

Wolsey, 34, 39, 45

Wren, 176